Tailored resour

MAKE THE GRADE

WJEC GCSE English and English Language

Barry Childs

Ken Elliott

Nick Duncan

Stuart Sage

Spoken language consultant:
Jane Hingley

Higher

www.pearsonschools.co.uk

✓ Free online support
✓ Useful weblinks
✓ 24 hour online ordering

0845 630 22 22

Heinemann

Part of Pearson

Heinemann is an imprint of Pearson Education Limited, a company incorporated in England and Wales, having its registered office at Edinburgh Gate, Harlow, Essex, CM20 2JE. Registered company number: 872828

www.pearsonschoolsandfecolleges.co.uk

Heinemann is the registered trademark of Pearson Education Limited

Text © Pearson Education Limited 2010

First published 2010

14 13 12 11
10 9 8 7 6 5 4

British Library Cataloguing in Publication Data
A catalogue record for this book is available from the British Library on request.

ISBN 978 0 435 01687 6

Designed and produced by Kamae Design, Oxford
Cover design by Wooden Ark Studios, Leeds
Picture research by Sally Cole
Cover photo © Gaertner/Alamy
Printed in Malaysia, CTP-KHL

Acknowledgements
We would like to thank the schools that were involved in this project for their invaluable help creating exam answers for this book.

The author and publisher would like to thank the following individuals and organisations for permission to reproduce photographs:

p7 EDDIE KEOGH/Reuters/Corbis; p9 Clynt Garnham Lifestyle/Alamy; p10 David Lichtneker/Alamy; p14 John Foxx/Getty; p16 Getty Images; p17 Ashley Cooper/CORBIS; p20 (background) Mark William Penny/Shutterstock; p20 (foreground) ALEXIS ROSENFELD / SCIENCE PHOTO LIBRARY; p23 Scott Barbour/Getty Images; p26 Clive Brunskill/Getty Images Sport; p27 AP Photo/EFE, Carlos Fdez; pp28–29 James Leynse/Corbis; p31 Robert Houser/Photolibrary.com; p35 Roy Rainford/Robert Harding/Rex Features; p37 The Telegraph Newspaper; pp39, 76, 83 David Collister; p43 Travelpix Ltd/Getty Images; p45 Christopher Nicholson/Alamy; p47 (top) George Standen/Alamy; p47 (middle) David Jackson/Alamy; p47 (bottom) David Lyons/Alamy; p53 Zuma Press/Press Association Images; p55 Daniel Atkin/Alamy; p57 BBC; p63 Getty Images; pp64–65 Joe Klamar/AFP/Getty; p70 Kunst & Scheidulin/Photolibrary; p72 Mike Harrington; pp74–75 Bill Stormont/CORBIS; pp80, 83 Ian Walton/Getty Images Sport; pp84–85 Getty Images; p89 Andrew Miksys/Getty Images; pp90–91 Janine Wiedel Photolibrary/Alamy; p93 Wataru Yanagida/Getty; p97 Arieliona/Shutterstock; p99 Keith Morris/Alamy; p101 Anthony West/Corbis; p106 Jack Sullivan/Alamy; p114 Getty Images; p120 Andrew Holt/Alamy; p126 FSG/Photolibrary; p132 JoeFox/Alamy; p134 CHARLES DHARAPAK/Staff; p138 Sally and Richard Greenhill/Alamy; p141 (film poster) c.Warner Br/Everett/Rex Features; p144 Leon/Retna Ltd/Corbis; p151 Mel Yates/cultura/Corbis; p153 Ben Radford/Corbis; p157 Neil Fraser/Alamy; p158 Ian Shaw/Alamy; p163 Andrew Fox/Alamy; p167 Geoff du Feu/Alamy.

Every effort has been made to contact copyright holders of material reproduced in this book. Any omissions will be rectified in subsequent printings if notice is given to the publishers.

Extract from *A Walk in the Woods* by Bill Bryson, published by Black Swan. Reprinted by permission of the Random House Group Ltd; Extracts from the Captive Animals website are used with kind permission of The Captive Animals' Protection Society. www.captiveanimals.org; Extract from 'The Day of the Eco-Pests' by Paul Vallely, from *The Daily Telegraph* © 06/07/1993. Used by permission of The Telegraph Media Group Limited; Extract from *The Road To Wigan Pier* by George Orwell © George Orwell, 1937. Reprinted by permission of Bill Hamilton as the Literary Executor of the Estate of the Late Sonia Brownell Orwell and Secker & Warburg Ltd and A. M Heath & Co. Ltd; 'Rubbish Attitudes Laying Waste to Our Landscapes' by John Ingham from *The Daily Express* © 08/05/2005. Used by permission of Express Newspapers; Extract from 'Aquarium Fish Suffer Abuse and Ill Health' by Severin Carrell from *The Independent* © 26/09/2004. Used by permission of The Independent News and Media Limited; 'Heart-throbs of the High Sea' by Emma Cowing from *The Scotsman* Living Section © 17/10/2006. Used by permission of The Scotsman; 'The sunshine isle where teenage tearaways are sent to learn a lesson' by Lucie Morris from *The Daily Mail* © 08/05/2007. Used by permission of The Daily Mail and Solo Syndication; 'How I spent £15 million on the Garden' by Rachel Cooke from *The Sunday Telegraph* © 30/09/2001. Used by permission of Telegraph Media Group Limited; 'We've Seen No One Since We Set Off…' by Cassandra Jardine from *The Telegraph* © 16/12/2005. Used by permission of Telegraph Media Group Limited; 'Fastest Lady on Two Wheels!' by Petronella Wyatt from the Daily Mail © 05/08/2007. Used by permission of The Daily Mail and Solo Syndication; Extract from *Notes from a Small Island* by Bill Bryson, published by Black Swan. Reprinted by permission of The Random House Group Ltd; Leaflet on Llandudno, used by kind permission of Conwy County Borough Council; The Blackpool Zoo leaflet has been used with kind permission of the Blackpool Zoo; Extract from 'Katherine Legge: Racing Driver' by Fabienne Williams from *The Observer* © 17/12/2007. Used by permission Guardian News & Media Ltd; Oxfam Leaflet 'I'm in' is reproduced with the permission of Oxfam GB, Oxfam House, John Smith Drive, Cowley, Oxford, OX4 2JY, UK www.oxfam.org.uk. Oxfam GB does not necessarily endorse any text or activities that accompany the materials; Extract from article 'What Can be Said now in defence of this sport?' by Niall Hickmann from *The Daily Mail* © 1998. Used by permission of the Daily Mail and Solo Syndication; 'Please will you stop paying to have my people murdered?' Campaign Advertisement from Friends of the Earth. Used with permission; 'We're Worth Every Penny' by Jay Curson, 19/10/2002 from *The Guardian*. Used by permission of the Guardian. Copyright © Guardian News & Media Ltd 2002; 'It's a Mad, Mad, Mad World' by David Hunn from *The Times* © 05/06/1994. Used by permission of The Times and NI Syndication; Leaflet 'The Benefit of Recycling Food Waste' from Pembrokeshire County Council; Book Review 'The Other Half Lives' from *The Times* © 05/09/2009. Used by permission of the Times and NI Syndication; Book Cover for *The Other Half Lives* by Sophie Hannah © 2009. Published by Hodder & Stoughton. Used by permission of Hodder Headline; Review of *Whiteout* by Anthony Quinn from *The Independent* © 11/09/2004. Used by permission of The Independent News and Media Limited; Review of *Draw the Line* by Andy Gill from *The Independent* © 11/09/2004. Used by permission of The Independent News and Media Limited; Cover of *Draw the Line* by David Gray, produced by Polydor. Used by kind permission of Universal Music Company; 'Isn't this the sort of jail Britain needs?' by Joanna Walters from the *Daily Express* © 01/08/2008. Used by permission of Express Papers; 'Prison Boot Camps prove no sure cure' by Ian Fisher from The *New York Times* © 10/04/1994. Used by permission of The New York Times and Pars International; Amended 'Vegetarian Society' Logo. Used by kind permission of the Vegetarian Society; Logo from 'Lloyds TSB' by Lloyds TSB. Used with kind permission; Playstation logo used with kind permission. PlayStation and the Sony Computer Entertainment logo are registered trademarks of Sony Computer Entertainment inc; Logo from Penguin books used by kind permission of Penguin Books; Extract from WJEC DVD, is used by kind permission of WJEC.

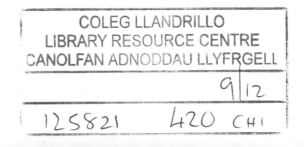

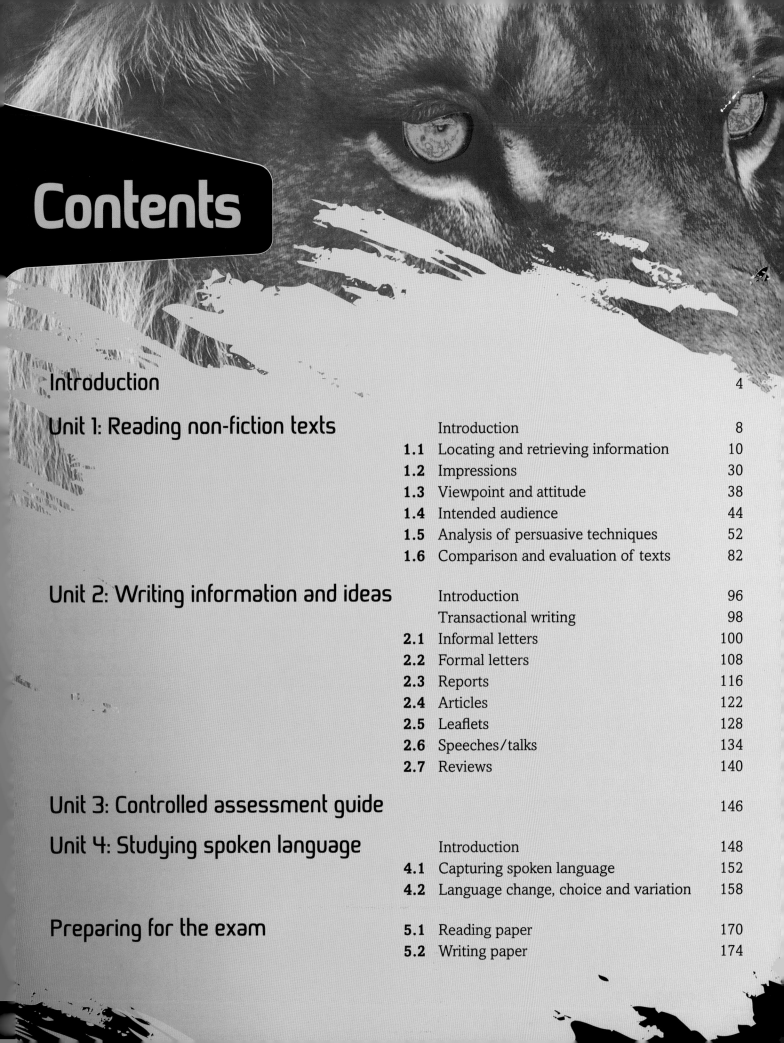

Contents

Introduction for students

This book is designed to help you raise your achievement in the WJEC GCSE English and GCSE English Language higher tier exams and controlled assessment tasks. It is tailored to the requirements of the specifications to help you improve your grades.

The book is divided into the following units:

▶ Unit 1: Reading non-fiction texts

▶ Unit 2: Writing information and ideas

▶ Unit 3: Controlled assessment guide

▶ Unit 4: Studying spoken language

▶ Preparing for the exam

How does this book work?

Each unit is divided into sections which cover the assessment objectives and requirements of the exams.

Each section is then broken down into lessons, most of which opens with its own learning objectives ('My learning objectives'). The lessons teach the skills you need to do well in the exam.

GradeStudio, contained within the lessons, provides an opportunity to read sample student answers and tips from senior examiners on how to move up through the grades and put what you have learnt into practice.

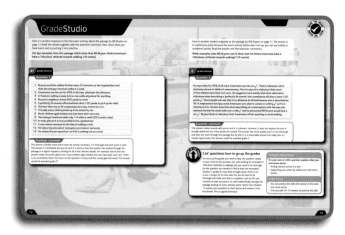

Many of the lessons provide an opportunity for you to grade yourself in the 'Peer/ Self-assessment' activity. Here you can reflect on what you have learnt and begin to understand how to move up the grades.

The approach of this book builds on many years of examining experience, workshops, training sessions and revision courses with teachers and students. It can be used with confidence to help you develop and achieve the best grades you can.

We hope you enjoy using this book and find it useful in developing your skills. Good luck in the exams.

What is in the exams?

You will have to take two exams in order to complete either GCSE English or GCSE English Language. These are as follows:

	Paper 1: Reading non-fiction texts	**Paper 2: Writing information and ideas**
How long is the exam?	1 hour	1 hour
What is in the exam?	There are two passages to read – a media text and a non-fiction text. There will be four or five questions on the texts, each carrying ten marks. One of the questions will ask you to compare the texts in some way. Occasionally there will be two questions worth five marks and three worth ten marks each.	There are two tasks to complete, both of which will be transactional/discursive in nature e.g. letters, reports, articles, leaflets, reviews. Each task will be marked out of 20 so you should divide your time equally. Across the two tasks you will be asked to write for a range of audiences and purposes.
How much should I write?	It depends on the size of your handwriting, but aim to write about half to one side for each answer.	It depends on the size of your handwriting, but aim to write one to two sides for each answer.
How will I be assessed?	All exams have what is known as 'assessment criteria', which define what is being tested by the questions.	
What is the assessment criteria?	**Assessment Objective 2** • Read and understand texts, selecting material appropriate to purpose, collating from different sources and making comparisons and cross-references as appropriate. • Develop and sustain interpretations of writers' ideas and perspectives. • Explain and evaluate how writers use linguistic, grammatical, structural and presentational features to achieve effects and engage and influence the reader.	**Assessment Objective 3** • Write clearly, effectively, using and adapting forms and selecting vocabulary appropriate to task and purpose in ways which engage the reader • Organise information and ideas into structured and sequenced sentences and paragraphs using a variety of features to give clarity and cohesion to your work • Use a range of sentence structures for clarity, purpose and effect, with accurate punctuation and spelling. *NB One third of the marks for each writing activity is allocated to this last bullet point.*

What is in controlled assessment?

For GCSE English, in your written controlled assessment you will be asked to complete the following activities:

▶ an essay linking a Shakespeare play and poetry. For this piece, you may write about any Shakespeare play and a range of poetry from the WJEC Poetry Collection

▶ an essay on a Different Cultures prose text taken from the GCSE English Literature set text list. Your teacher will tell you which text you are studying

▶ a piece of first-person writing

▶ a piece of third-person writing.

For GCSE English Language, in your controlled assessment you will be asked to write:

▶ an essay on a novel or play taken from the GCSE English Literature set text list or any play by Shakespeare (except the two listed in the GCSE English Literature set text list). Your teacher will tell you which text you are studying

▶ a piece of descriptive writing

▶ a piece of narrative/expressive writing.

For both GCSE English and GCSE English Language, you will have to complete three Speaking and Listening assignments:

▶ Communicating and adapting language (probably an individual presentation)

▶ Interacting and communicating (probably group work)

▶ Creating and sustaining roles (role-play).

If you are taking GCSE English Language, you will also have to complete a spoken language study.

You will find more information about controlled assessment on pages 146–147. Unit 4 (pages 148–169) will help you with the skills needed for the spoken language study.

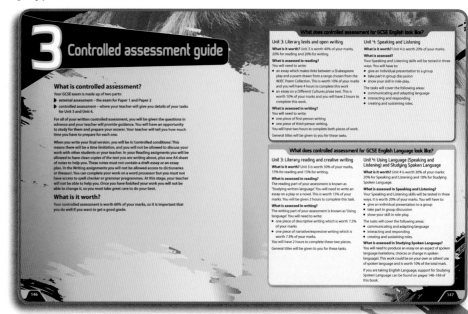

For teachers

What additional resources are there?

▶ **Teacher Guide** with full-colour lesson plans and schemes of work, written by experienced WJEC teacher and Head of English, Sarah Donnelly. These lesson plans make use of the BBC footage and other resources in the ActiveTeach CD-ROM as well as providing support for EAL students. There is also additional controlled assessment guidance for teachers, written by Stuart Sage and Nick Duncan.

▶ **ActiveTeach CD-ROM** an on-screen version of the student book together with BBC footage and other resources including grade-improvement interactive activities, handouts and the full Teacher Guide.

1 Reading non-fiction texts

What will the Reading paper look like?

In the Reading paper you will have to read two examples of non-literary texts on a common theme. These could be an advert, a factsheet, a newspaper or magazine article, a page from the Internet, a leaflet or an essay (e.g. travel writing).

Each year the exam includes different texts in different combinations, so you cannot predict what will be used. Also, it is highly unlikely that you will have read the material before.

What will the questions be like?

The questions fall into different, but quite predictable, categories. The trick is to recognise the type of question and what it requires. You need to prepare yourself by practising the types of questions you are likely to be asked, and you should use a range of different kinds of material. For example, a leaflet is different from an essay, and you need to be confident about how to approach the various kinds of material. This section of the book is designed to help you to do exactly that.

The wording of the questions varies from year to year and you cannot be certain which questions will appear. However, only **six** basic types of question are asked in this exam. Examples of these appear on page 9. If you practise answering them, you should be well prepared and able to face the exam with confidence.

What should I do?

You have one hour to complete this paper, so there is no time to waste. First, you could read the two texts. This will take some time, so alternatively, you could just read the text you need to answer the opening one or two questions. You then only need to read the second text when you reach the question(s) on that text. Only the last question will require you to consider both texts.

How will I be assessed?

The examiner will assess your answers against the assessment criteria outlined on page 5.

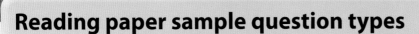

Reading paper sample question types

Below are some examples of the types of question you could be asked in the Reading paper. These will help you understand what you are preparing for as you work through this section of the book.

1 Locating and retrieving information

- List reasons or details/Make a list of…
- According to this text or writer, how or what or why…?
- What evidence does the writer use…?
- Explain how and/or why…

2 Impressions

- What impressions do you get of the writer?
- What impressions do you get of an organisation or people?
- What impressions do you get of a place?

3 Viewpoint and attitude

- What are the writer's attitudes to…?
- What are the writer's opinions of…?
- What are the writer's thoughts and feelings about…?

4 Intended audience

- Who is this text aimed at?

5 Analysis of persuasive techniques

- How does the writer try to encourage/interest/argue?
- How does this text try to persuade/sell/influence/show?

6 Comparison of texts

- Compare and contrast these texts.
- Using information from both texts, explain why…

Flintoff: 'I'd do anything to play'

THE TIMES

£50bn cash

'List or find' questions

My learning objectives ▼

- to select relevant details from a passage
- to present details clearly using a list or prose.

Questions that ask you to locate and retrieve information do not always appear on the Higher Tier paper, but if they do, they are usually opportunities to gain marks quickly, provided you read the passage carefully and closely.

How to tackle a 'List or find' question

When you are asked a '**List or find**' question, you need to:

▶ work your way through the passage in a methodical way

▶ look carefully for the relevant points and underline or highlight them as you go.

This will make sure that the material is clear for you to use when you have to write your answer, and you may not need to read it again.

GradeStudio

Examiner tips

- If you are asked to 'make a list' or 'list...' then you should do exactly that.
- If you are asked for ten points (or the question has 10 marks), include eleven or twelve if you can: you may have got something wrong or made the same point twice, but an extra point or two gives you a safety net.

Activity 1

Use the above method when you answer the following sample questions from the exam.

1   The first question requires a response in a list.

Read the extract opposite by Bill Bryson. The question on this extract is:

List <u>ten</u> examples from this passage which show that Bill Bryson thinks Americans have a 'ridiculous' attitude towards walking. (10 marks)

2   Now look at the following question which asks for the same information in a different form:

What examples does Bill Bryson use to show that he thinks Americans have a 'ridiculous' attitude towards walking? (10 marks)

Notice that the second question does not say that you can use bullets or numbered points: this time you should write a paragraph using continuous prose. It would be unwise to use numbered or bullet points unless you are told that you can.

3   Compare your responses with those in GradeStudio on pages 12–13. Which grade is your answer closest to? How can you improve?

Now here's a thought to consider. Every twenty minutes on the Appalachian Trail, Katz and I walked further than the average American walks in a week. For 93 per cent of all trips outside the home, for whatever distance or whatever purpose, Americans now get in a car. That's ridiculous.

5   When we moved to the States one of the things we wanted was to live in a town, where we could walk to the shops and post office and library. We found such a place in Hanover, New Hampshire. It's a small, pleasant college town, with big green, leafy residential streets, an old-fashioned main street. Nearly everyone in town is within an easy level walk of the centre, and yet almost no-one walks anywhere, ever,

10 for anything. I have a neighbour who drives 800 yards to work. I know another – a perfectly fit woman – who will drive 100 yards to pick up her child from a friend's house. When school lets out here, virtually every child gets picked up and driven from a few hundred yards to three-quarters of a mile home. (Those who live further away get a bus.) Most of the children sixteen years or older have their own

15 cars. That's ridiculous too. On average the total walking of an American these days – that's walking of all types – adds up to 1.4 miles a week, barely 350 yards a day.

    At least in Hanover we can walk. In many places in America now, it is not actually possible to be a pedestrian, even if you want to be. I had this brought home to me in Waynesboro […] when I left Katz at a launderette […] and set off to find some

20 insect repellent for us. […]

    Waynesboro had a vaguely pleasant central business district but, as so often these days, most retail businesses have moved out of town leaving little but a sprinkling of dusty second hand shops in what was presumably once a thriving downtown.

    Lots of shops were dark and bare, and there was nowhere I could find to get

25 insect repellent, but a man outside the post office suggested I try K-mart.

    'Where's your car?' he said, preparatory to giving directions.

    'I don't have a car.'

    That stopped him. 'Really? It's over a mile, I'm afraid.'

    'That's OK.'

30   He gave his head a little dubious shake, as if disowning responsibility for what he was about to tell me. 'Well, then what you want to do is go up Broad Street, take a right at the Burger King and keep on going. But, you know, when I think about it, it's *well* over a mile – maybe a mile and a half, mile and three quarters. You walking back as well?'

35   'Yeah.'

    Another shake. 'Long way.'

    'I'll take emergency provisions.'

    If he realised this was a joke he didn't show it.

    'Well, good luck to you,' he said.

Extract from *A Walk in the Woods* by Bill Bryson

GradeStudio

Here is a student response to the first exam activity about the passage by Bill Bryson on page 11. Read the answer together with the examiner comment, then check what you have learnt and try putting it into practice.

List <u>ten</u> examples from this passage which show that Bill Bryson thinks Americans have a 'ridiculous' attitude towards walking. (10 marks)

A* grade answer

Question 1

1. Bryson and Katz walked further every 20 minutes on the Appalachian trail than the average American walks in a week.
2. Americans use the car for 93% of all trips, whatever the distance.
3. In Hanover, walking is easy but no-one walks anywhere for anything.
4. Bryson's neighbour drives 800 yards to work.
5. A perfectly fit woman will sometimes drive 100 yards to pick up her child.
6. The fact that she is 'fit' emphasises how lazy Americans are.
7. Virtually every child is picked up from school by car.
8. Most children aged sixteen and over have their own cars.
9. The average American walks only 1.4 miles a week (350 yards a day).
10. In many places it is not possible to be a pedestrian.
11. A man seems shocked at the idea of walking a mile.
12. He takes the joke about 'emergency provisions' seriously.
13. He wishes Bryson 'good luck' as if he is setting out on a trek.

Examiner comment

This answer includes more points than are strictly necessary. It is thorough and each point is clear. The answer is methodical and precise and it is obvious that the student has worked through the passage in a logical sequence, looking for all of the relevant details. For example, notice how this answer makes the point about how 'most children aged sixteen and over have their own cars'. There is no uncertainty there. The focus on the question is sharp and this would gain full marks. This answer would be awarded grade A*.

Here is another student response to the passage by Bill Bryson on page 11. The answer is in continuous prose because the exam activity below does not say you can use bullets or numbered points. Read the answer and the examiner comments.

What examples does Bill Bryson use to show that he thinks Americans have a 'ridiculous' attitude towards walking? (10 marks)

C grade answer

Question 2

He says that for 93% of all trips Americans use the car ✓. 'That's ridiculous' which obviously shows he thinks it unnecessary. Also he says it is ridiculous that most of the children have their own cars. He suggests more subtly that their attitude is ridiculous when describing a 'perfectly fit woman' who sometimes will drive a mere 100 yards ✓. Most people can see this is no distance at all and because she is described as 'fit' it emphasises how lazy some Americans are when it comes to walking ✓ and how ridiculous it is. He also does this when describing his conversation with the man who seemed shocked he would walk over a mile ✓ and he presumed Bill Bryson would have a car ✓. Bryson finds it ridiculous that Americans will do anything to avoid walking.

Examiner comment

This answer makes several valid points and it is coherent. However, it does not explore the text in enough detail and too many points are missed. The answer has some quality, but it is not thorough and does not work through the passage line by line. It is a reasonable answer, but really this is a missed opportunity. This answer would be awarded grade C.

'List' questions: how to go up the grades

To move up the grades you need to keep the question clearly in your mind (in this question you were looking for examples of 'ridiculous' attitudes to walking) and you need to be thorough (in this question you needed to find at least ten examples). Student 1 packed in more than enough points. There is no virtue in length for its own sake, but you do need to be thorough and make sure that in a question such as this you mention at least ten points. So, work methodically through the passage, looking for every relevant point. Notice how Student 1's answer uses quotation in short pieces and weaves it into the answer. This is a good technique.

Putting it into practice

On your own or with a partner, explain what you now know about:
- finding relevant points in a text
- supporting your points by reference to the text's details.

In the future

- You can practise this skill with several of the texts you come across.
- Give yourself 10–15 minutes to practise this skill.

My learning objectives ▼
- to practise selecting relevant details
- to develop a secure approach to 'List or find' questions.

'List or find' questions ask you to find relevant material and present it in a particular way. Now it is your turn to practise a 'List or find' question.

GradeStudio

MAKE THE GRADE ✓ MAKE THE GRADE

Examiner tips

- Be methodical, relevant and thorough.
- Remember that bullet points should make sense.

Activity 1

Read the extract and answer the question below. The extract is taken from a factsheet produced by CAPS (The Captive Animals' Protection Society).

List the criticisms which CAPS makes of zoos. (10 marks)

Sad Eyes & Empty Lives

In the wild, animals react to their surroundings, avoiding predators, seeking food and interacting with others of their species – doing what they have evolved for. Consequently, even what might seem 'larger' or 'better' enclosures may be […] impoverished in terms of the animals' real needs.

5 Frustration and boredom are commonplace amongst animals in zoos and can lead to obsessive and repetitive behaviours in the form of pacing, swaying, and even self-mutilation. This is known as stereotypic behaviour and such pointless, repetitive movements have also been noted in people with mental illnesses. With nothing to do, animals in zoos go out of their minds. Disturbed maternal behaviour may involve over-
10 grooming and the rejection or killing of young. […]

Even diets are unnatural, with zebras in zoos becoming overweight as the grass they are given is higher in calories than the grasses of the African savannah. The resulting obesity can affect fertility. […]

Some animals suffer such serious behavioural problems in zoos that they are given
15 anti-depressants, tranquillisers and anti-psychotic drugs to control their behaviour.

Zoos often refer to the animals they confine as being 'ambassadors' of their species, but just what message does it give when we see animals in such unnatural conditions, displaying disturbed behaviours?

From The Captive Animals' Protection Society

Activity 2

Read the extract and answer the question below.

According to this article, what actions has Carmen Glatt taken to show her concern about pollution and the environment?
(10 marks)

The day of the Eco-Pests
By Paul Vallely

Adults are unwise to try drinking water from the tap while Carmen Glatt is around. Carmen is only eleven but nobody could question her clarity of vision or her determination. She is very aware that
5 all the water we drink is recycled, says her mum, and she is convinced that anything which comes out of a tap must be polluted in some way. She conscientiously changes the family's water filter every week.
10 'If someone gets a drink of water from the tap she says "No, No, No" and throws it away and gets some from the filter. She washes all salad and fruit with filtered water,' says her mother. As a nutritionist, Mrs Glatt is no slouch on health matters but she
15 admits she is no match for her daughter [...]
And it is not just the water. There is air pollution too. 'She even bought a breathing filter for her father for when he cycles to the office,' says Mrs Glatt, clearly both simultaneously overwhelmed
20 and impressed by her daughter's tenacity. 'And he has to buy unleaded petrol,' she adds.
When it comes to shopping Carmen accompanies her mother to the supermarket to supervise the family purchases. 'She reads the packages of
25 everything and watches out for certain chemicals or artificial sweeteners. She won't have certain kinds of apples because she says they taste of chemicals.'

The Daily Telegraph

GradeStudio

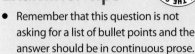

Examiner tips

- Remember that this question is not asking for a list of bullet points and the answer should be in continuous prose.
- Be methodical and thorough and make every sentence of your answer count.

Peer/Self-assessment

1 Check your answers to Activities 1 and 2.
  - Did you find enough clear points?
  - Did you present and organise your answer in the appropriate way?

2 Now try to grade your answer to Activities 1 and 2 by applying what you learnt in GradeStudio. You will need to be careful and precise in your marking.

Tick each clearly made, supported point. For a question like this, the total number of ticks will produce, or strongly influence, the final mark.

⬆ Moving up the grades

A*	9/10 ticks
A	8 ticks
B	7 ticks
C	5/6 ticks
D	4 ticks

My learning objectives ▼

- to select relevant evidence from a passage
- to organise the evidence into a coherent response.

'Evidence' questions

If you are asked to find evidence, it is important that you work your way through the passage in a methodical way. All passages – Internet articles, leaflets, newspaper articles and so on – have been carefully chosen and edited, so always study the relevant lines in detail. It is likely that almost every sentence is making a point or saying something that is worth including in the answer.

Activity 1

Read the exam question below and the passage that follows it.

What evidence does Orwell use to suggest that Sheffield was a dreadful place? (10 marks)

The key pieces of evidence in the text have been underlined to show you how to work on a passage and make a good selection of relevant details.

1 Use the text to produce an answer and practise integrating short pieces of text into your response.

The passage below was written by George Orwell in 1937 after he visited the industrial north of England.

Sheffield, I suppose, could justly claim to be called the ugliest town in the Old World: its inhabitants, who want it to be pre-eminent in everything, very likely do make that claim for it. It has a population of half a million and it contains fewer decent buildings than the
5 average East Anglian village of five hundred. And the stench! If at rare moments you stop smelling sulphur it is because you have begun smelling gas. Even the shallow river that runs through the town is usually bright yellow with some chemical or other. Once I halted in the street and counted the factory chimneys I could see; there were
10 thirty-three of them, but there would have been far more if the air had not been obscured by smoke. One scene especially lingers in my mind. A frightful patch of waste ground […] trampled bare of grass and littered with newspapers and old saucepans. To the right an isolated row of gaunt four-roomed houses, dark red, blackened by smoke. To
15 the left an interminable vista of factory chimneys, chimney beyond chimney, fading away into a dim blackish haze. Behind me a railway embankment made of the slag from furnaces. In front, across the patch of waste ground, a […] building of red and yellow brick […].
　　At night, when you cannot see the hideous shapes of the
20 houses and the blackness of everything, a town like Sheffield assumes a kind of sinister magnificence. Sometimes the drifts of smoke are rosy with sulphur, and serrated flames, like circular saws, squeeze themselves out […] of the foundry chimneys.

From *The Road to Wigan Pier* by George Orwell

1 Now try the question below about the following extract.

   What evidence does John Ingham use to show the scale of the problem of litter and waste? (10 marks)

2 Compare your responses with those in GradeStudio on pages 18–19. Which grade is your answer closest to? How can you improve?

Daily Express

Rubbish attitudes laying waste to our landscapes

From the hedgerows of Cornwall to the country lanes of Cumbria, our green and pleasant land is under threat – not from alien species threatening to devour our native flora and fauna but from a mountain of waste.

Wherever you look, our beautiful landscape is defaced by rusting fridges, plastic bags, clapped-out cars, fast-food litter, old prams, tyres […].

The plague of illegal dumping has become so bad in my corner of rural Surrey, we find ourselves ringing the council to get rubbish removed on an ever-increasing basis. According to Keep Britain Tidy, it costs local authorities more than £400 million to clean up litter each year.

We live in a consumerist, throwaway society in which it seems to be the norm to get rid of cars, furniture and electrical appliances within a couple of years of buying them. Is your two-year-old computer a bit slower than the new ones on the market? Dump it. Is your mobile phone clumpy and old-fashioned? Dump it, along with the other 90 million cluttering up the country. Get a trendy one.

And everything we buy, from chocolate to computers, comes swaddled in layers of paper, plastic and cardboard which could be recycled but is more likely simply to be chucked out.

Each year, homes and businesses throw away 100 million tons of rubbish – enough to fill Trafalgar Square to the top of Nelson's Column every day. Some of it is dealt with sensibly and responsibly. Increasingly, though, it is simply dumped in our streets, on our verges and in our fields.

GradeStudio

Here are three student responses to the exam question below about the article by John Ingham on page 17. Read the answers together with the examiner comments, then check what you have learnt and try putting it into practice.

What evidence does John Ingham use to show the scale of the problem of litter and waste? (10 marks)

E grade answer

Student 1

In the newspaper article there is a lot of evidence used to show the size of the problems of litter and waste in Britain. The writer refers to lots of big companies in the text, for example, 'According to Keep Britain Tidy, it costs local authorities more than £400 million to clean up litter each year'. ✓

The numbers used could shock the reader and hopefully make them think twice before throwing a piece of litter on the floor. Big numbers and statistics are used quite a lot in this text, the writer talks of dumping your mobile phone 'along with the other 90 million cluttering up the country' ✓ and how each year '100 million tons of rubbish are thrown away.' ✓

Examiner comment

Student 1's answer is short and, although it begins by claiming there is 'lots of evidence' to show the size of the problem of litter and waste, it does not actually find much at all. The claim that the text refers to 'lots of big companies' is a complete mystery, and 'Keep Britain Tidy' is not a company. However, the answer does mention the cost of cleaning up the litter. The next paragraph does not answer the question and drifts into the effect of the text on the reader. The final paragraph is better and picks up two more relevant pieces of evidence, but there are only three in total and that means a maximum grade of E.

B grade answer

Student 2

John Ingham uses this evidence to show the size of the problems of litter and waste in Britain. He says that it costs 'more than £400 million to clean up litter each year'. ✓ Homes and businesses throw away '100 million tons of rubbish' ✓ which is enough to 'fill Trafalgar Square up to the top of Nelson's Column'. ✓ He tells us 'increasingly, rubbish is simply dumped in our streets, verges and in fields' ✓ and he suggests that rubbish is 'everywhere' from 'Cornwall to Cumbria'. ✓ He calls it a 'mountain of waste' ✓ that defaces our beautiful landscape. He says that '90 million mobile phones' ✓ clutter up our countryside.

Examiner comment

Student 2's answer is not long but the focus on the question is good and this is a sound answer. Several valid points are made but some are missed, which could be a result of a rather disorganised approach. The answer does not track the text in a logical sequence and there is always a risk that points will be missed if you dart here and there. There is nothing wrong in this answer, but it is not thorough or efficient enough in gathering the evidence to gain the highest marks. It would get grade B.

A* **grade answer**

Student 3

John Ingham suggests this problem is nationwide from Cornwall to Cumbria ✓ and the waste is 'a mountain', suggesting its large scale. ✓ He claims that rubbish is everywhere. It is 'wherever you look'. ✓ He then lists the items that litter the 'beautiful' countryside such as 'rusting fridges, plastic bags and old prams' ✓ and uses the word 'plague' to suggest that litter is spreading like an infectious disease. ✓ He uses personal experience (calling the council every week) ✓ and the shocking statistic of £400 million just to clean up the litter. ✓
He describes Britain as 'consumerist and throwaway', a place where it is 'normal' to get rid of items before they are really useless. ✓ 90 million 'dumped' phones is a staggering statistic ✓ and he draws attention to all the packaging on consumer items. This packaging, he claims, is likely to be 'chucked', not recycled. ✓ 100 million tons of rubbish thrown away each year by homes and businesses is another dramatic statistic, ✓ and the reference to filling Trafalgar Square to the top of Nelson's Column is a dramatic illustration of the scale of the problem. ✓ He ends by insisting that there is increasing dumping on verges, streets and fields. ✓

Examiner summary

This answer is totally focused on the question and it finds the evidence in a clear and thorough way. It is easy to follow and it has fluency and coherence. Working methodically through the text seems to ensure comprehensive coverage and misses nothing. You might notice that some explanation is offered where it is considered necessary, but the focus on the question is never lost. The key skill is to select enough relevant material from the text. This answer would gain full marks and reach a grade A*.

'Evidence' questions: how to go up the grades

To move up the grades you should begin by working your way through the text carefully but quickly, using a pen or a highlighter to mark the relevant points.

Keep the question firmly in mind and don't get distracted in the way that Student 1's answer does. Sometimes a little explanation is sensible, but you do not have time to get bogged down in making one point at great length. Keep a sense of momentum: you only have limited time so you must keep moving through the text. Practise weaving the text fluently into your writing and keep the quotations short. Stay in a logical sequence to avoid the disorganised approach which undermined Student 2's answer. Make sure that you have covered the specified section of the text and found as much relevant material as possible.

Putting it into practice

On your own or with a partner, explain what you now know about:
- finding evidence in a text
- using the text in your answer
- organising your answer
- including any necessary explanation
- what makes the difference between a grade B answer and a grade A* answer.

In the future

- Make sure that you practise this type of question with several texts.
- Get used to marking the text quickly and using what you have found.
- Practise the technique of weaving the text into your answer.
- Work towards producing a complete answer in 10–15 minutes.

My learning objectives ▼
- to practise selecting relevant evidence
- to develop a secure approach to this type of question.

Exam practice and assessment

When answering 'Evidence' questions, you need to work methodically through the text, underline (or highlight) the relevant points and use them neatly in your answer. Now it is your turn to practise this type of question.

Activity 1

Read the extract and answer the question below.

What evidence do CAPS and the RSPCA use to show that marine animals are badly treated in aquariums? (10 marks)

CAMPAIGNERS REVEAL ILL-TREATMENT OF CAPTIVE MARINE CREATURES

By **SEVERIN CARRELL**

Thousands of fish and animals in Britain's aquariums are suffering sickness, distress and physical abuse, a damning report by animal rights campaigners has
5 revealed.

The investigation found that dozens of aquariums keep animals such as rays, sharks, puffer fish, crabs and squid that are scarred and deformed, behave
10 abnormally, or are routinely mishandled by staff and visitors.

Video footage released by the Captive Animals' Protection Society (CAPS) […] shows a starfish which had lost a limb
15 through being manhandled, children throwing diseased crabs into pools, sharks being held out of their pools to be touched, and staff forcing rays to swim out of the water to feed. Rays and sharks
20 in more than 20 aquariums showed abnormal behaviour such as 'surface breaking', where they poke their heads above the water, often because they are 'trained' to feed that way.

Peer/Self-assessment

1 Check your answers to Activity 1.
  - Did you find enough clear points?
  - Did you present and organise your answer in the appropriate way?
2 Now try to grade your answer to Activity 1 by applying what you learnt in GradeStudio. You will need to be careful and precise in your marking.

You should tick each clearly made and supported point and for a question like this the total number of ticks will produce, or strongly influence, the final mark.

Moving up the grades

A*	9/10 ticks
A	8 ticks
B	7 ticks
C	5/6 ticks
D	4 ticks

THE INDEPENDENT

The society also claims that few aquariums 25 are involved in genuine marine conservation work, challenging a key marketing claim by most of the businesses involved. CAPS alleges that more than 80% of aquarium animals are caught in the wild and are very rarely used 30 in breeding programmes to save endangered species.

The allegations […] are a serious blow to the reputation of Britain's aquariums, which are key attractions in many seaside towns. 35 They now attract millions of visitors each year, and the number of aquariums has leapt from one in the late 1970s to an estimated 55 today.

The CAPS findings […] have been backed by 40 the Royal Society for the Prevention of Cruelty to Animals. Its marine scientific officer, Laila Sadler […] said tens of thousands of fish die in British aquariums each year while thousands die in transit to them. RSPCA experts, she said, 45 'very frequently' see malnourished and ill fish at aquariums. Claims that aquariums actively support marine conservation programmes are a 'convenient veneer', she added. 'There is a disposable attitude to these animals […] we're 50 losing tens of thousands of fish every year in Britain. The costs to these animals are never, never exposed in these places.' […]

The CAPS allegations are likely to shock many of Britain's marine conservation 55 groups.

My learning objectives ▼

- to learn how to approach 'Explain' questions
- to practise explaining a writer's ideas and perspectives.

'Explain' questions

'Explain' questions require the skill of selecting relevant information, but in Higher Tier more is required than 'search and find'.

▷ There is usually a need to provide some explanation to give the answer clarity and coherence.

▷ There are often opportunities for inference and overview and the best answers combine those skills with a good selection of supporting detail from the text.

Inference skills

What you have to do in this type of question is to show that you have read and understood what a text is saying. There are several levels of understanding in most texts and you need to show that you have grasped the surface meaning but also that you can read between the lines and see the deeper ideas which are implied by what is said. This is called inference and it is a key skill in moving you up the grades.

To detect inference you will probably have to follow an argument. This means that you must stay in sequence to see the direction the writer is taking. You need to use your vocabulary precisely to show that you have understood what you have read and then provide as much textual support as you can in the time available.

Read the brief extract below. It is the opening of an article about Ben Fogle, a television presenter, and James Cracknell, an Olympic gold medallist in rowing. In 2005 they had competed in a race to row across the Atlantic Ocean.

The exam question was as follows:

Explain how women react to Fogle and Cracknell, according to this extract. (10)

Glossary

ardour enthusiasm

Heart-throbs of the High Seas

BY EMMA COWING

'What lovely boys!' exclaims a woman in a tweed suit, eyes riveted to a desk on the far side
5 of the main foyer of the Glasgow Royal Concert Hall. Another woman totters past on the arm of her teenage son, pouting grumpily. 'Never mind, Mum,' he
10 consoles her, 'maybe you'll get a kiss next time.' In the corner, a small gaggle of excited female staff has assembled, just to gaze.
The subjects of all this **ardour**
15 are sitting behind a large table signing books, oblivious to the commotion they might be causing. Or maybe they're just used to it. Because when Ben
20 Fogle and James Cracknell walk into a room [...], ladies swoon. When they appeared on stage earlier to discuss their recent adventure, you could almost
25 hear the rustle as 400 women simultaneously started rooting in their bags for lipstick.

THE SCOTSMAN

1 Use a table like the one below to assemble your answer to the exam question. You need to do two things:
- find key quotations from the text that show how the women react (evidence)
- for each quotation, say what point is being made (inferences).

There are three main points to make here, but you should be able to find at least seven pieces of evidence to support your answer. The table has been started for you.

Evidence	Inferences
1 A woman calls them 'lovely boys'	Women are attracted to them
2 Her eyes are 'riveted' to them	
3 A woman is disappointed and 'grumpy' when she does not get a kiss	

When you have completed your table, pull together the evidence and inferences you have made and show that you understand the main points by using some of your own words in your answer.

2 Now read the student answers in GradeStudio on pages 24–25. What evidence and inferences has each student used in their answer? Which grade is your work above closest to? How can you improve?

GradeStudio

Check your answers

- Did you find enough evidence from the text?
- Did you manage to say something about the evidence you found?
- Are you sure that you have got the main points clear?

GradeStudio

Here are two student responses to the exam activity below about the article on page 22. Read the answers together with the examiner comments, and then check what you have learnt and try putting it into practice.

Explain how women react to Fogle and Cracknell, according to this extract. (10 marks)

Student 1

In the first line a woman exclaims 'What lovely boys!' ✓ This already suggests that the women have reacted well to the men. Further down a young daughter of a woman consoles her and says 'maybe you'll get a kiss next time'. This indicates that women reacted so well that they wanted more than a signed book. ✓ Furthermore, it says that when Ben Fogle and James Cracknell walk into a room 'ladies swoon'. ✓ This also implies that women like the lads. As well as this the fact that '400 women' gather in the same room as the lads, ✓ suggests that they have set an impression on the women. And in the last line it says how the women look for lipstick ✓ tells me that the women have reacted very well to these brave young men.

Examiner comment

Student 1 spots a range of relevant material but it is limited, mainly because it lacks the vocabulary to explain precisely. The suggestion that women 'reacted well' to these 'lovely boys' is weak and the misreading of 'daughter' for 'teenage son' is careless. The next point is well made and it is true that the women seemed to want 'more than a signed book' from the men. The extract tells us that 'ladies swoon' when the men enter a room but it is not enough to say that this implies 'women like the lads.' The point that Fogle and Cracknell can attract an audience of 400 women could have been convincing, but the lack of precision is evident in the weak claim that they have 'set an impression' on women. The final point about the lipstick is made simply and without any depth of understanding. This is a reasonable answer but it lacks the sharpness and coherence to be more than grade C.

A* **grade answer**

Student 2

Women are obviously very attracted ✓ to Fogle and Cracknell. One woman calls them 'lovely boys' ✓ and her eyes are 'riveted' ✓ to them. Another woman is 'grumpy' and disappointed ✓ because she did not get a kiss and has to be 'consoled' by her son. ✓ They are the centre of attention ✓ and a crowd of female staff are 'excited' ✓ and 'gaze' at them. ✓ The men cause a 'commotion' among their female admirers ✓ who are said to 'swoon' when they walk into a room. ✓ Women want to impress ✓ the two men and an audience of 400 women were 'simultaneously rooting for their lipstick' ✓ when they appeared on stage.

Examiner comment

This answer uses the text well and takes the opportunity to add some explanation and show understanding by making inferences. It is a clear answer and works methodically through the text, gathering credit as it goes along. This answer misses nothing and would gain full marks. Grade A*.

Explain questions: how to go up the grades

To move up the grades you need to show that you have understood what is being said in the text and to keep a clear focus on the question. In this question you were asked to explain 'how women react' to the two young men and you needed to see the main points and use evidence from the text to support your answer.

The first answer does spot a reasonable range of relevant points in the text but it lacks the precise vocabulary to explain carefully what those points are suggesting to the reader.

The second answer shows you clearly how to do it. It is thorough in its use of the text and it uses quotation in short pieces which are woven into the answer without interrupting the sense or the flow. The inferences are clear and precise and the answer scores consistently. Notice that this ability to use quotation and mix it with accurate comment is the key to the A* answer.

Putting it into practice

On your own or with a partner, explain what you now know about:

- using evidence from the text to show you have understood what you have read
- linking the evidence to inferences to show your understanding
- what makes the difference between a grade C answer and a grade A* answer.

In the future

- Make sure you practise this skill using a variety of texts.
- Try to link evidence from the text to inferences.
- Aim to produce complete answers in 10–15 minutes.

My learning objectives ▼

- to practise 'Explain' questions
- to learn how to combine evidence and inference.

Exam practice and assessment

Examiner tip

This question asks you to explain why the two men took part in the race. Look at each man's reasons in turn. They **may** have had similar reasons but not necessarily, so don't be too quick to say 'They', unless you are absolutely sure the point refers to both men.

When answering 'Explain' questions, remember to look for the relevant evidence and try to say something to develop the point and show your understanding. Try to be as precise as possible in your choice of words.

Now it is your turn to practise this type of question.

Activity 1

Read the extract opposite, which is the next section of the article about Fogle and Cracknell. Use a table like the one below to help you plan your answer. Then write your answer to the question.

Explain why Fogle and Cracknell took part in this race.
(10 marks)

Fogle	Cracknell

The pair had spent 49 days rowing the Atlantic in a tiny 20ft-long boat, winning the world's toughest rowing race despite having spent
5 only four months preparing (the average is two years) [...]. Most people, it is fair to say, thought they were mad. [...]

Fogle [...] has presented a
10 number of TV programmes, including *Animal Park* and *Cash in the Attic* [...]. Unlike Cracknell, a professional rower and two-time Olympic gold medallist, he had
15 no real experience in the sport. So why do something so extreme? [...] 'It gives you a huge buzz.'

Later on though, he admits there may have been other
20 reasons driving his decision. 'If there was a psychologist here I'm sure he'd say it was a symptom of not wanting to be seen as "Ben Fogle, presenter of *Cash in the*
25 *Attic*",' he says. 'There is a lot more to me outside of that little sphere.'

Cracknell had only recently won his second gold medal at the Athens Olympics when he
30 bumped into Fogle at a cocktail party. When Fogle – at the time a complete stranger to the Olympian – seized his opportunity and asked if he would be interested
35 in rowing the Atlantic, his answer was an emphatic 'no'. But, over time, the idea grew on him. In the end, his choosing to sign up came, in part, from confusion over his
40 future career. [...]

[...] Cracknell says, 'Stopping sport is an incredibly tough thing. I've had so many brilliant opportunities to do different
45 things since I stopped, but if anyone asks what I'm doing now, nothing sounds as worthwhile as "I'm training for the Olympics." You get away with four years of
50 having everything done for you, working to a routine, being like Peter Pan really – you don't have to grow up.'

Cracknell thought he could use
55 the time away from the e-mail, the mobile and the pressures of everyday life to think things through, and make a final decision on whether or not to go
60 to Beijing.

GradeStudio

Examiner tips

MAKE THE GRADE ✓

- The key to this question is how well the answer follows an argument. It must have some fluency and make sense.
- Make sure that your answer is as **clear and precise** as you can make it.
- Include as much evidence as you can, but remember to comment where you can.

Activity 2

On page 17 you read the first part of an article by John Ingham on the problem of waste and litter in Britain. Below is the next section of his article, where he argues that the problem is likely to get worse. Read the article and answer the exam question below.

Explain carefully why, according to John Ingham, the problems of rubbish and litter are likely to get worse. (10 marks)

This mountain of waste could become a range of Alpine proportions over the coming years. First, retailers are locked in a
5 bitter struggle to woo customers – and that means glitzier packaging. Second, a series of European Union regulations designed to protect the environment will almost certainly
10 trigger more fly-tipping.

The rules requiring ozone-thinning chemicals to be taken out of fridges have already led to a spate of fridge dumping by
15 owners who fear having to pay for them to be taken away. And we can expect to see more electronic goods sprouting from ditches as EU law will require the toxins they
20 contain to be removed and then the rest recycled. The number of cars dumped – currently 350,000 a year – is also likely to increase. EU law treats old cars as toxic waste
25 and demands they be disposed of by a specialist industrial plant. Car dumping was already on the up because of the collapse of the price in scrap metal. Not so long
30 ago, dealers would pay you to take your old banger away; now they are not interested, or you have to pay them.

For all my suspicions about meddling by the EU, these laws 35 are a good thing. The problem lies in making sure they are enforced. So far, governments have failed.

Take Britain's appalling record on recycling. Last year Britain 40 recycled just 12% of waste. Switzerland, Austria, Holland and Germany recycle about 50% of their

Daily Express

waste. Even America, the world's worst polluter, manages about 31%.

In Britain we continue to bury our rubbish out of sight and out of mind.

If it's not recycled, the rubbish has to buried or burned. Both options are unattractive. Dangerous chemicals can leak from landfill sites into the water supply and incinerators release all sorts of cancer-causing chemicals into the air. Yet this is the choice facing us unless we are prepared to make changes in our behaviour.

Peer/Self-assessment

1 Check your answers to Activities 1 and 2.
- Did you use evidence from the text?
- Did you say something about the evidence you found?
- Are you sure that you have got the main points clear?
- Did you follow the text in a clear sequence?
- Did you keep the quotations short and integrate them into your answer?
- Did you use your own words to make inferences?
- Did you think carefully about the words you used?
- Did you have an overall sense of the writer's argument?

2 Now try to grade your answer to Activity 2 using the mark scheme below. You will need to be careful and precise in your marking. Use the mark scheme to help you.

Give a tick for each clear inference and a tick for each piece of relevant evidence. The ticks will guide you to the correct mark but you also need to make a judgement about the quality and coherence of the answer.

⬆ Moving up the grades

A 8–10 marks
- ▶ selects and analyses a range of valid points
- ▶ best answers are thorough and coherent with some depth of understanding and overview.

C 5–7 marks
- ▶ spots a range of valid points
- ▶ better answers have a clear focus on the question and a sense of coherence.

D 2–4 marks
- ▶ makes simple comments
- ▶ spots some surface features of the text
- ▶ better answers have a focus on the question.

My learning objectives ▼

- to understand how texts attempt to present an impression of their subject
- to learn how to approach this type of question.

'What impressions?' questions

Sometimes a question in the Reading paper asks what **impression** an article or a factsheet creates of an organisation, an individual, a place or group of people. This simply means the view you might have of the person or organisation when you read what is being said about them.

Activity 1

1   Read the newspaper article below. What impression does the writer create of teenagers?

2   List any words or phrases that help to create this impression, and say what image they suggest. For example, if you think the impression is a negative one, the use of the word 'tearaways' in the headline suggests they are out of control.

THE SUNSHINE ISLE WHERE TEENAGE TEARAWAYS ARE SENT TO LEARN A LESSON

By Lucie Morris

With its cooling palms and spectacular views of the nearby mountains, it is an idyllic holiday destination.

5   This Caribbean paradise is also the playground of a group of notorious teenage tearaways.

While their hard-working classmates shiver in the cold and rain 10 back home, the seven are spending two weeks in the sun, enjoying swimming, tennis and trips to the sights of Jamaica, as part of a scheme organised by the Divert Trust.

15   The five boys and two girls, aged 13 to 16, who come from Nottingham, are considered the most disruptive pupils at their three schools.

All face expulsion after 20 consistently skipping classes, disrupting lessons, disobeying teachers and breaking school rules.

Many failed to do their homework or show any commitment to school 25 work and school activities.

'Nobody knows what to do with them,' a school governor said last night. 'But sending them on a free holiday is not the answer.'

30   'What kind of message does this give out to other children when they see the way these children have been given such a special treat?'

The youngsters are staying at a 35 former hotel built in 1888 in a suburb of the capital Kingston and now used as a Roman Catholic convent and school complex for 1400 children.

Just a few miles away are soft 40 white beaches lapped by the bluest of oceans.

The Divert Trust, a charity which offers support to children at risk from school exclusion, has footed the full 45 £5000 bill for the trip and claims it will be 'highly beneficial'.

Chief executive Angela Slaven insisted yesterday: 'They will have to study at schools, talking to people 50 and experiencing how children in Jamaica learn. This is certainly not a holiday.'

The pupils have a full programme of events for their stay, which 55 includes visits to schools and cultural institutions.

The organisers hope what they see will encourage them to value

3 Use your list from question 2 to help you answer the exam question below.

What impressions does this newspaper article create of the seven teenagers on the Divert Trust scheme? You must use the text to support your answer. (10 marks)

Daily Mail

their education and respect authority
60 after seeing how Jamaican children are committed to their school work, despite the fact that many have few resources and live in poverty.

The tearaways will also enjoy days
65 out at the Dunn's River Falls tourist attraction and a museum dedicated to reggae legend Bob Marley.

Outraged parents and governors condemned the venture as an insult
70 to better-behaved classmates.

A governor at the school which two of the seven attend, said the school was 'very annoyed' at the decision to take them away.
75 She added: 'We were not informed about the trip and we

hadn't sanctioned it. I really didn't agree with almost rewarding badly-behaved children.'
80 At the convent, run by the Mission of the Immaculate Conception, the children are closely supervised but are still able to enjoy the expansive grounds and playing fields.
85 Sister Celia Cools-Lartigue said: 'They are enjoying their stay. They are a bit noisy at times but otherwise not too bad.

'They have a packed schedule
90 every day and will be taking lots of trips.

'They sleep in dormitories and have two good meals a day. They seem to be fussy eaters, though
95 – we don't really know what to feed them. They don't seem to like English or Jamaican food.'

The trip was originally aimed at 19 pupils who were set individual
100 targets for achievement, but only seven performed well enough to secure a place.

GradeStudio

Here are two student responses to the exam question below about the article on pages 30–31. Read the answers together with the examiner comments, then check what you have learnt and try putting it into practice.

What impressions does this newspaper article create of the seven teenagers on the Divert Trust scheme? You must use the text to support your answer. (10 marks)

Student 1

Relevant quotation from the text.

Point developed sensibly.

Neat quotations are well integrated.

Valid point with textual support.

The newspaper article describes the seven teenagers as 'a group of notorious teenage tearaways'. From this statement we are immediately given the impression that these children are always up to no good and don't think about the consequences of their actions. The article goes on to explain that they are the 'most disruptive' and 'all face expulsion'. This does not make the seven pupils sound as if they deserve a holiday, as one governor has pointed out 'a free holiday is not the answer'. Everything that is said about the seven teenagers or 'tearaways' does not create a good impression and many people are said to be outraged. This makes the article sound quite aggressive and it reflects badly on the teenagers.
The writer often refers to them as 'tearaways', 'disruptive' and 'badly behaved'. These references are constantly keeping up the bad impression we are given of them. The Divert Trust scheme is said to be 'a charity which offers support to children at risk from school exclusion'. This does not commend the charity, but highlights that these children have behavioural problems.

Vague comment.

Spots some phrases but not developed.

Losing a little focus.

Unclear but hinting at something here.

Examiner comment

This answer begins sensibly with a direct reference to the teenagers, and the opening sentence keeps a tight focus on the question. The comment that follows ('these children are always up to no good') also gains reward, but the answer then becomes repetitive and towards the end loses some focus on the teenagers; there is not enough to reward in the final sentences and they are not making a significant contribution to the answer. Overall, it misses quite a few of the details. This is a grade B answer.

A* grade answer

Student 2

The article describes the teenagers as 'notorious' and 'tearaways', which gives the impression that they are rebellious against the school system in Britain. They are described as 'disruptive' and they all 'face expulsion', which conveys the idea that nobody knows what to do with them. They are accused of 'disobeying teachers' and 'breaking school rules', which gives the impression that they have no respect for anything or anyone. The pupils are labelled as 'tearaways' which gives the impression that they are hard to control and have totally broken away from any civilised discussions about their behaviour. They are 'notorious' and this conveys the idea that they are well-known for their bad behaviour. The teenagers are described as beyond help when a school governor says 'Nobody knows what to do with them.' They are also described as 'fussy eaters' which shows that they are ungrateful for the holiday, which they did not deserve in the first place.

Examiner comment

This answer immediately selects some key words used to describe the teenagers and then says clearly what impression is created by those words. This technique is pursued and the textual evidence is used well to prompt a series of clear impressions. There is some repetition of 'notorious' and 'tearaways' but the impressions are correct and do not repeat the opening. The focus on the question never falters and the grasp of what impressions the writer is trying to create is excellent. It is purposeful and perceptive. This is an A* answer.

'What impressions?' questions: how to go up the grades

To move up the grades, you need to keep a clear focus on the question and search carefully through the text to find the relevant facts and the choices of words and phrases which create the impressions. Quotations are important, but they are not enough on their own. You must make it clear what impressions you get and then use the text as support to prove your points. **Do not give up after one or two impressions**. There will always be at least five or six separate points to make, so stick with the text and work your way through in sequence.

Putting it into practice

On your own or with a partner, explain what you now know about:
- finding impressions in a text
- supporting your impressions by reference to the facts given in the text
- supporting your impressions by selecting and analysing key words and phrases.

In the future

- You must practise this type of question using a range of texts.
- Always start with an 'impression' (how you see something or someone).
- Use facts and words/phrases to support your answer.
- Make sure you include at least five or six impressions.
- Aim to produce a complete answer in 10–15 minutes.

My learning objectives ▼

- to practise 'What impressions?' questions
- to develop a secure technique for answering these questions.

When answering 'What impressions?' questions, remember that you must offer at least five or six impressions and support each one with facts and words/phrases from the text.

Now it's your turn to answer this type of question.

Activity 1

Read the question below and the extract that follows it.

What impressions of the Duchess of Northumberland do you get from Rachel Cooke's article? (10 marks)

How to spend £15 million on a garden

By RACHEL COOKE

In 1996, the Duchess of Northumberland, Jane Percy, announced that a splendid, but hugely expensive, garden would be created in the grounds of Alnwick Castle, the stronghold of the Percy family since the Middle Ages. The garden would be a haven for adults and a playground for children, including educational facilities. It would bring visitors to the town and boost the local economy.

Jane's husband, Ralph, set up a charitable trust and handed over £5 million of family money to set her on her way; Tim Smit, the driving force behind the Eden Project in Cornwall, gave his blessing; and the Prince of Wales agreed to be the project's patron. The locals, however, were less than impressed. Who, they chorused, does she think she is – Marie Antoinette?

On the way to my hotel in Alnwick, the taxi driver filled me in. He said the Duke and Duchess believed they just had to click their fingers and everyone else would come running – even the local water board. Some months before, the town's high street had been dug up so that the castle's water supply could be improved (fountains will feature prominently in the garden). Several businesses complained that passing trade fell, and so did takings. For a town getting back on its feet after the foot and mouth crisis, it was hard to bear.

The man who put me up for the night, however, had a different story. The Duchess's garden would, he insisted, do the town nothing but good. He was about to add more bedrooms in readiness for all those who would come to see the garden. Jane Percy was, he said, a decent, determined woman with few airs and graces. 'You'll like her,' he added, giving me a stern, protective look. 'It's hard not to.'

As it turned out, he was right. I went to Alnwick feeling cynical; I came away planning to visit again. The Duchess is still largely surrounded by mud and men in hard hats, but she has the look of a woman with a hunch that she is about to be vindicated. She defies anyone not to fall in love with the garden when it is complete, however disapproving they may have been in the past.

'I suspect it's human nature for people to be critical,' she says as we stand in the garden, mugs of tea in our hands and ready to put on fluorescent workmen's jackets. She has a girlish voice and a self-deprecating manner; she prefers combat pants to tweeds, and her Geordie workmen all call her Jane.

'I suspect, too, that I'm always going to be a target,' she continues. 'It's very character-building. I suppose I should try to win the critics round, but actually I can't

The Sunday Telegraph

be bothered. It's not my garden. I'd be a bit pathetic if I was building this huge thing just for myself.'

Jane Percy, daughter of an Edinburgh stockbroker, never expected to be a duchess, nor to live in a medieval fortress sufficiently large and gloomy to be chosen to play the part of Hogwarts in the Harry Potter films. Her husband inherited his vast estate unexpectedly on the death of his older brother. Ralph and Jane, who had met as teenagers, were living in a farmhouse with their four children. 'It was difficult for me to leave the farmhouse but we knew we had a duty to Alnwick,' says Jane, the first Percy duchess from outside the ranks of the aristocracy. 'The trouble was, the castle was like a cross between a hospital and a museum. It didn't seem like a home at all.'

To help ease the transition, the Duke suggested that his wife should take charge of the gardens but the Duchess has been dogged by criticism from those who failed to see why the Percys did not fund the whole thing themselves. She has had to remind her critics that the family do not have unlimited cash. She says, perhaps not sounding too convincing, 'we still have the same worries about our credit card bills as anyone else.'

The Duchess is quick to remind me that any profits will go straight back into the project. 'The family can't make a penny out of the garden. We can't even get our original 5 million pounds back.'

Her project is the most ambitious garden to be created in Europe for a century, and tomorrow is the day when all her ambitions will be put to the test. The designers have gathered together 65,000 hardy plants to cope with the cold Northumbrian climate but the central theme is water. As the Duchess puts it, visitors will see 250,000 gallons of the stuff 'going absolutely bananas'. The cascade – a technological miracle – is the central feature and she says 'I have this nightmare that we'll press a button and 250,000 gallons of water will rush down the cascade, fail to stop at the bottom and drown everyone and everything in their path.'

Activity 2

Below is a 'What impressions?' question. Try it out on your own and assess your progress with the advice in the Peer/Self-assessment box opposite.

What impressions does James Cracknell give of what it was like to take part in this race? (10 marks)

In 2005, James Cracknell, an Olympic gold medallist in rowing, and Ben Fogle, a television presenter, entered a race to row across the Atlantic in a small boat. James Cracknell gave an interview by telephone when they were about one thousand miles into the race.
5 *This is what he said.*

Since last Saturday, we have hardly made any progress – just 100 miles in almost a week. We've experienced the worst weather they've ever had in the race and it looks as if it will continue until next Tuesday.

10   The hurricane itself didn't hit us, but we got caught by strong winds blowing in exactly the wrong direction so we had to put down the sea anchor. For two and a half days, we were stuck in our cabin, which is like being shut in a car boot. When the wind eased off, we were able to set off at midnight and row for seven hours,
15 which took us over the 2000 miles-to-go mark. We celebrated with a chocolate bar. But we keep having to stop because of the weather.

    We've lost so many days that we are starting having to ration our food. We wanted to do the race in 40 days and took enough food for 50, but that looks optimistic now, so we've cut our daily ration
20 of 8000–9000 calories by 500–600. By the time we get to the last few days, we will be having a horrible time because we've left all the food we don't like until then.

    We've been thirsty as well as hungry. Earlier in the week, the **desalinator** broke and we nearly had to break into the fresh water
25 we carry as ballast. […] We could only drink five to six litres a day, instead of ten.

    We haven't seen another boat since the day we set off so we don't know our position in the race, but I expect others have pulled ahead […]. The weather has brought out the differences in our
30 competitive attitudes, so there has been a bit of tension. I mind about being overtaken and I'm keener to row in the rain than Ben is; he just wants to get to the end.

Glossary

desalinator a machine that removes salt from seawater

GradeStudio

Examiner tips

- The key to this question is how well the answer follows an argument. It must have some fluency and make sense.
- Make sure that your answer is as clear and precise as you can make it.
- Include as much evidence as you can, but remember to comment where you can.

GradeStudio

Check your answers

- Did you find at least six impressions?
- Did you find some evidence to support the points you made?
- Did you look for the 'facts'?
- Did you pick out some particular words and phrases?

I'm not looking forward to the next four days because we're going to be stuck in the cabin again. We're bored with talking to each other, we've only got one pack of cards and we've played all the games we know. 35

We need to sleep as much as we can, but it gets really hot in the cabin because the wind is so strong that we have to keep the windows and hatch shut. Out of a twelve-hour night, we probably sleep for only two hours, and spend the rest of the night trying to get comfortable. We sleep head to toe on a shelf that is only the width of a shoulder and, just as I am dozing off, I find Ben's foot in my mouth. 40 45

Peer/Self-assessment

1 Check your answers to Activities 1 and 2.
   - Did you find at least six impressions?
   - Did you work through the text in a sequence?
   - Did you find facts in the text to support your impressions?
   - Did you find any examples of particular words and phrases used by the writer?

2 Now try to grade your answer to Activity 2 using the mark scheme below. You will need to be careful and precise in your marking. Give a tick for each clear impression and a tick for each piece of relevant evidence. The ticks will guide you to the correct mark, but you also need to make a judgement about the quality and coherence of the answer.

⬆ Moving up the grades

A 8–10 marks
▶ explores appropriate detail from the text with depth and insight
▶ best answers are thorough and perceptive, covering a range of points accurately and with an assured grasp of character.

C 5–7 marks
▶ selects appropriate detail from the text to show understanding of the situation (making inferences)
▶ better answers sustain a valid interpretation.

D 2–4 marks
▶ makes simple comments based on surface features of text
▶ shows awareness of straightforward implicit meaning.

My learning objectives ▼

- to understand how texts attempt to present a viewpoint or attitude towards their subject
- to develop an understanding of how to approach this type of question.

'Attitudes' questions

Writers often do more than present facts and information. They frequently want to present a particular view on the subject they are writing about, or persuade the reader. They may have a negative or positive attitude towards their subject and sometimes an exam question will ask you to explain what their attitude is and how this is made clear to the reader.

A question of this type may include the words 'attitude' or 'viewpoint' in it, but you are more likely to be asked to explain the writer's 'thoughts and feelings'.

When you answer this kind of question:

▶ It is useful to start your answer with reference to 's/he thinks' or 's/he feels'. It is not necessary to start every single sentence with these words, but it makes sense to return to them throughout your answer to ensure you are answering the question.

▶ Each thought or feeling you identify must be supported by evidence from the text.

▶ Stay in sequence and follow the text in a logical way so that you can see the way thoughts and feelings develop.

▶ Use the third person ('he' or 'she') in your answer. Avoid using the first person ('I think' or 'I feel'), as this will take you away from the question.

Activity 1

Read the article opposite and the question below. The question asks you to work out the author's attitudes to the challenge she is about to face. However, it is worded as follows:

What are Petronella Wyatt's thoughts and feelings as she prepares to ride the TT course? (10 marks)

The extract opposite was written by a journalist called Petronella Wyatt. She was about to ride around the TT course in the Isle of Man as a passenger on a motorcycle. This is the opening section of an article she wrote about the experience.

Create a table to help you plan your answer to the question. One has been started for you below. Then write your answer to the question.

Thoughts and feelings?	Evidence
She feels nervous and scared	She describes the TT course as 'infamous'
She thinks the American writer had it easy	It is the 'most dangerous' circuit in the world

Daily Mail

THE FASTEST LADY ON TWO WHEELS!

by Petronella Wyatt

The late American writer Hunter S. Thompson once compared riding a 1000cc motorbike round a hairpin bend to 'diving into a pool
5 and suddenly realising it has been emptied.' Hunter, you had it easy!

I am riding pillion at 120mph along the twisting mountain roads of the Isle of Man's infamous
10 TT course, the most dangerous motorcycle circuit in the world.

If I fall off, there isn't even any ground to hit. On my left is a 600ft drop into the sea. On the right, a
15 seemingly bottomless ravine. This is the mouth of death, these are the jaws of Hell. [...]

In what insane [...] moment did I agree to road test the TT course
20 before the professionals arrived? [...]

[...] Simon Crellin, who is helping to organise the race, has arranged for me to ride with a 2002 winner, Richard 'Milky' Quayle. 25

I have never ridden pillion on a powerful motorbike before, let alone at high speed, though I have occasionally driven scooters in Italy – up to 10mph, usually from 30 a dress shop to a nearby café (on one occasion I forgot to brake and drove through a café). I dare not tell Simon of my inexperience, however, lest I be sent home in 35 disgrace.

He must sense something is amiss, though, for he is a little surprised by my outfit, which consists of kitten heels and a 40 leather skirt.

'I think we'd better fit you for some proper leathers,' he says, when we meet in my hotel lobby. 'Are you sure you have ridden a 45 powerful machine before?'

'Oh, yes,' I say, thinking of the time I rode a bucking bronco at a fair and fell off. [...]

Early the next morning, Simon 50 introduces me to Milky. [...] He is on the weedy side, with watery eyes and a pale face with a dreamy expression. [...]

[...] We go over and look at the 55 bikes. They are monstrous. [...]

Fortunately, I see a smaller, safer-looking machine in the corner that resembles more of a motorised bicycle. 'I'll ride that one,' I say. 60

'But that's a 1907 bike,' protests Simon. 'It only goes up to 25mph.'

'That's why I'll ride it.'

Here are two student responses and examiner comments to the exam question below about the article by Petronella Wyatt.

What are Petronella Wyatt's thoughts and feelings as she prepares to ride the TT course? (10 marks)

C grade answer

Student 1

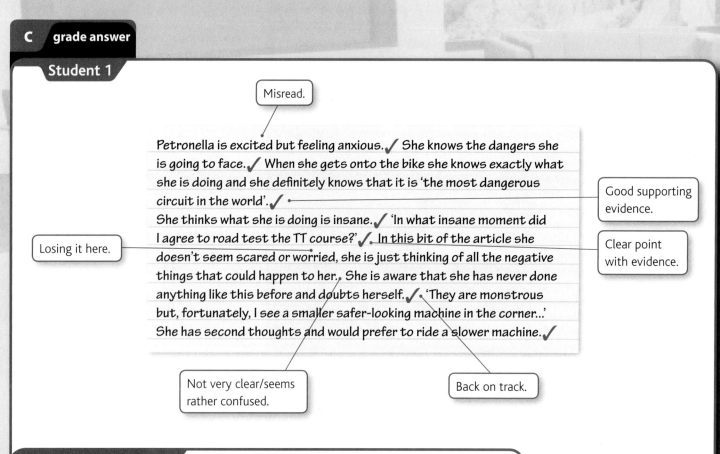

Misread.

Petronella is excited but feeling anxious. ✓ She knows the dangers she is going to face. ✓ When she gets onto the bike she knows exactly what she is doing and she definitely knows that it is 'the most dangerous circuit in the world'. ✓

Good supporting evidence.

She thinks what she is doing is insane. ✓ 'In what insane moment did I agree to road test the TT course?' ✓ In this bit of the article she doesn't seem scared or worried, she is just thinking of all the negative things that could happen to her. She is aware that she has never done anything like this before and doubts herself. ✓ 'They are monstrous but, fortunately, I see a smaller safer-looking machine in the corner...' She has second thoughts and would prefer to ride a slower machine. ✓

Clear point with evidence.

Losing it here.

Not very clear/seems rather confused.

Back on track.

Examiner comment

This answer gets off to an uneasy start but recovers quickly and then makes a series of sensible points with some support from the text. The second paragraph starts well but then gets confused before getting back on track. It is an uneven answer, and it does not see the subtleties, but it sees enough to justify a grade C.

Student 2

Petronella is feeling challenged ✓ at the thought of her drive. This is shown when she claims that the American writer who compared riding a fast motorcycle to diving into an empty pool 'had it easy'. ✓ She is feeling worried ✓ as she writes 'if I fall off, there isn't any ground to hit', which suggests she thinks she might. ✓ She is feeling scared as she describes the '600ft drop into the sea' and 'bottomless ravine'. ✓ It is obvious she is terrified of the deadly consequences ✓ of doing this as she describes the course as 'the mouth of death' and the 'jaws of hell'. ✓

She is thinking it was a bit stupid to agree to do this as she thinks 'in what insane moment did I agree to road test the TT course?' ✓

Petronella questions her ability to do the course as she writes 'I have never ridden pillion on a powerful motorbike before. ✓ She is feeling inexperienced ✓ but also unprepared ✓ as she has turned up in 'kitten heels and a leather skirt'. She is thinking just how little experience she has on fast machines as she remembers the time she rode a 'bucking bronco at a fair and fell off'. ✓

She is worried she won't be safe with Milky as he is 'on the weedy side'. ✓ She is shocked by the 'monstrous' bikes ✓ but feels safer and relieved at the prospect of riding a 'smaller, safer looking machine'. ✓

Examiner comment

This answer begins well and gets better and better. There is clear understanding here and each point is supported by a good choice of textual evidence to clinch what is being said. There is absolutely no misreading here and it goes well beyond just 'scared' and 'nervous' to include her feelings of being stupid, unprepared, inexperienced, shocked and relieved. It even includes her feelings about Milky. What makes this such a good answer is its clarity of understanding, range of reference and good support from the text. It is not particularly long, but it is totally focused on the question and keeps returning to 'thinks' and 'feels' to stay in position. This gets 10 marks: a clear A* answer.

'Attitude' questions: how to go up the grades

To move up the grades you need to keep a clear focus on the question and search carefully through the text to find a range of 'thoughts and feelings' or 'attitudes'. The quotations and details from the text are important, but they are not enough on their own. You must make clear what 'attitudes' the writer is getting across to you and then use the text as support to justify, or prove, your points. Do not give up after one or two thoughts or feelings; there will always be **at least** five or six separate points to make, so stick with the text and work your way through in sequence. Following a sequence is particularly important in this type of question.

Putting it into practice

On your own or with a partner, explain what you now know about:
- finding the writer's 'attitudes' or 'thoughts and feelings' in a text
- supporting your ideas by reference to the text
- supporting your ideas by selecting and analysing key words and phrases
- what makes the difference between a grade C answer and a grade A* answer.

In the future

- You must practise this type of question using a range of texts.
- Always start with a 'thought' or 'feeling'.
- Use textual evidence to support your answer.
- Make sure you include a range of thoughts and feelings.
- Follow the text in sequence.
- Aim to produce a complete answer in 10–15 minutes.

My learning objectives ▼

- to practise 'Attitude' questions
- to develop an understanding of how to approach this type of question.

Exam practice and assessment

When you are answering an 'Attitude' question, you must keep your focus on the writer's 'attitudes' or 'thoughts and feelings'. It is sensible to use 'he/she thinks or feels' as a way of staying in focus on the question. Use evidence to support what you say, but remember that details and quotations from the text are not enough on their own.

Now it's your turn to answer an 'Attitude' question.

GradeStudio

Examiner tips

- You should spend no more than 13–14 minutes on this question.
- Do not waste time and words. This question is not asking for your views.
- Follow what the writer is saying step by step, selecting relevant material.
- Each thought or feeling needs to be clearly linked to evidence in the text.
- Use the words of the question as your 'way in'.
- Include as much evidence as you can, but remember that it is not enough on its own.
- The key to this question is to identify a range of thoughts and feelings.
- Make sure that your answer is focused on the question. Use 'he/she thinks or feels' (it really does work).

Activity 1

Read the extract below and answer the following exam question.

What are Bill Bryson's thoughts and feelings about Blackpool? (10 marks)

Blackpool – and I don't care how many times you hear this, it never stops being amazing – attracts more visitors every year than Greece and has more holiday beds than the whole of Portugal.[…]

Whatever you may think of the place, it does what it does very
5   well – or if not very well at least very successfully. In the past twenty years, during a period in which the number of Britons taking traditional seaside holidays has declined by a fifth, Blackpool has increased its visitor numbers by 7 per cent and built tourism into a £250-million-a-year industry – no small achievement when you
10 consider the British climate, the fact that Blackpool is ugly, dirty and a long way from anywhere, that its sea is an open toilet, and its attractions nearly all cheap, provincial and dire.

It was the illuminations that had brought me there. I had been hearing and reading about them for so long that I was genuinely
15 keen to see them. So, after securing a room in a modest guesthouse on a back street, I hastened to the front in a sense of some expectation. Well, all I can say is that Blackpool's illuminations are nothing if not splendid, and they are not splendid. There is, of course, always a danger of disappointment when you finally
20 encounter something you have wanted to see for a long time, but in terms of letdown it would be hard to exceed Blackpool's light show. I thought there would be lasers sweeping the sky, strobe lights tattooing the clouds and other gasp-making dazzlements. Instead there was just a rumbling procession of old trams
25 decorated as rocket ships or Christmas crackers, and several miles of paltry decorations on lampposts. I suppose if you had never seen electricity in action, it would be pretty breathtaking, but I'm not even sure of that. It all just seemed tacky and inadequate on rather a grand scale, like Blackpool itself.

From *Notes from a Small Island* by Bill Bryson

Peer/Self-assessment

1 Check your answers to Activity 1.
   • Did you find a range of thoughts and feelings?
   • Did you work through the text in sequence?
   • Did you find evidence in the text to support each of your comments?
   • Did you find any examples of particular words and phrases used by the writer?

2 Now try to grade your answer to Activity 1 using the mark scheme below. You will need to be careful and precise in your marking. Give a tick for each clear 'thought' or 'feeling' and a tick for each piece of relevant evidence. The ticks will guide you to the correct mark, but you also need to make a judgement about the quality and coherence of the answer.

⬆ Moving up the grades

A 8–10 marks
   ▶ explores appropriate detail from the text with depth and insight
   ▶ best answers are thorough and perceptive, covering a range of points accurately and with an assured grasp of the writer's thoughts and feelings.

C 5–7 marks
   ▶ selects appropriate detail from the text to show understanding of the writer's thoughts and feelings
   ▶ better answers sustain a valid interpretation and stay focused on the question.

D 2–4 marks
   ▶ makes simple comments based on surface features of text
   ▶ shows awareness of straightforward implicit meaning
   ▶ some focus on the question.

My learning objectives ▼
- to understand how texts target particular individuals or groups of people
- to learn how to approach this type of question.

'Intended audience' questions

Questions on 'intended audience' are not often used in the exam, but they can be asked, usually in relation to advertisements. Questions are normally asking 'Who is this text aimed at?'.

If you are asked about intended audience, you have to work out who the specific targets are by looking at content and language. Let's look at an example.

Activity 1

Read the extract on the opposite page and answer the following questions.

1 The sub-heading immediately appeals to those who want to 'step back in time' and enjoy 'tranquil' surroundings.
   a What kind of people do you think this is appealing to?
   b What sort of things appeal to them?

2 Notice the mention of the attraction being close to the bus station.
   a Who would this be important to?
   b Do you think this is aimed at a particular group of people? Who are they?

3 The writer uses words such as 'delightful' and 'beautiful'.
   a Who would be attracted by this kind of language?
   b What are they looking for when they visit a place?

4 There is stress on the historical and royal associations of the place and the large collection of roses, described as 'exquisite' and 'astounding'.
   a What is the effect of these details?
   b Which particular 'interest' group has the writer got in mind?

5 The sea is mentioned, but notice it is not swimming or surfing, but the 'striking views' which are highlighted. The path is described as 'leisurely'. Who do you think this is appealing to?

6 The next paragraph talks of 'something to delight everyone', but perhaps by now you are thinking that this leaflet has a clear, and more specific, audience in mind.
   a Do you think it has something for everyone?
   b Who is this **not** aimed at?

7 Activities for children introduce another dimension to the leaflet.
   a Think carefully why they are mentioned.
   b Who is the target audience?

8 There is also attention to the disabled and a mention of the 'cosy and welcoming' tea room. This takes us back to the main audience for this leaflet.

Now, using what you have learnt, answer this question:

Who is this leaflet trying to attract to the Connaught Gardens? (10 marks)

THE CONNAUGHT GARDENS

A step back in time in tranquil surroundings

The seaside town of Sidmouth nestles between two great cliffs in picturesque Lyme Bay. It takes just five minutes' walk from the town's main bus station, along the Victorian-built Esplanade, to reach the Connaught Gardens from where there is a delightful view over the whole of the beautiful Regency town.

Named after the Duke of Connaught, the Connaught Gardens have associations with many royal figures, most notably Queen Victoria who frequently visited Sidmouth in her childhood. The Victoria Rose Garden, the pride of the Connaught Gardens, is dedicated to her memory and boasts an all-weather visitors' centre with exhibitions of photographs and clothes from the time, as well as an exquisite and astounding display of hundreds of different varieties of rose.

After you've looked at the original Victorian maps and manuscripts, a walk through the shady and scented orchard will take you to what locals call 'Paradise House', where exotic plants from all over the world will delight you as you walk along the sand. In winter there are free cider and apple juice tastings here, with the opportunity to take home a bottle all year round from the visitors' centre.

One of the things that makes Sidmouth truly special is its situation, right next to the clean blue sea. At the Connaught Gardens there are plenty of ways to enjoy the sea, from the Observation Terrace which affords striking views across Lyme Bay, to the winding path which leads leisurely down to the sandy beaches. Or why not take a walk down a small piece of history by walking down Jacob's Ladder, built in honour of Prince Albert by the brother of the distinguished engineer Isambard Kingdom Brunel.

There really is something to delight everyone at the Connaught Gardens. Children are encouraged to take part in the free activities held here during Sidmouth's annual folk festival, including dance, drama and art and crafts. Everywhere is suitable for wheelchair users and there is a full range of disabled facilities, including special seating for disabled people and their families in the Clock Tower Tea Rooms. Set in a real working clock tower with a brass bell, these tea rooms are cosy and welcoming, with plenty of menu choice. Why not try the delicious and traditional Devon Cream Tea, or perhaps a hearty slice of homemade cake?

Take a step back in time, effortlessly and in tranquil surroundings. We hope to see you soon!

THE CONNAUGHT GARDENS
Sidmouth

The advertisement opposite is trying to attract visitors to the seaside resort of Llandudno. You will notice that the pictures show children playing on the beach with buckets and spades, enjoying donkey rides and watching a Punch and Judy show. It would be tempting to jump to the conclusion that the advert is aimed at children, until you remember that small children do not actually make decisions about where to go for a day out or a holiday. A more accurate answer would be that this advert is aimed at parents, or families, with young children.

Activity 2

1 Look at the first four paragraphs of the text.
   - Make a list of the activities that would attract parents and young children.
   - Pick out any words or phrases you think are particularly effective.

   Two of the pictures reinforce the appeal to parents with young children, and your answer should include some reference to them. This is the most important audience for this advert, but it does have other targets.

2 Paragraphs 5–6 mention some 'fun events', including the 'waiter and waitress race' and 'people-watching'. Who do you think might be interested in those activities?

3 The final paragraph, which begins 'Neighbouring Llanfairfechan', is aimed at another group of people. Who exactly are they? What is mentioned to appeal to them?

4 Now look at the section at the bottom of the advert with the heading 'At a Glance'. Who is this section appealing to? How does the advert do this?

We have now identified at least four groups of people who are targeted by this advert, but it is definitely not aimed at 'everyone'. The group that is most obviously missing here is teenagers – there is really nothing here to appeal specifically to them!

Some students are quick to claim that adverts appeal to 'everyone'. In fact, advertisers are very skilful at aiming their advertisements at particular audiences. They think carefully about where and when they advertise their products and they target their audience in terms of things such as: age, gender, income and interests.

Where memories are made of sea, sand and fun

No childhood is quite complete without remembered dreams of halcyon days spent at the seaside, paddling in the waters or playing on the sands.

Llandudno has two beaches on either side of the town. The quieter West Shore with its long sandy beach and children's play area has wonderful views of the Conwy Estuary, Isle of Anglesey and Puffin Island, site of a Cistercian monastery.

North Shore is the lively beach, spanning the two-mile crescent bay for which Llandudno is famed.

Its popularity has stood the test of time. The traditional still thrives in the form of Punch and Judy shows, donkey rides and organised games. On the Pier there are stalls and amusements including Professor Peabody's Playplace with supervised activities for children. On the opposite end of the promenade, at Craig-y-Don, toddlers love splashing about in the paddling pool.

The promenade itself is a hive of activity during the glorious months of summer. There are fun events such as the charity pram race and bed-making competitions. The waiter and waitress race, a title keenly fought by the town's hotels, is in its 26th year. On balmy summer evenings listen to the sounds of local or visiting bands on the bandstand.

For fun and frivolity, sunbathing and people-watching, Llandudno is truly the place where memories are made.

Neighbouring Llanfairfechan, a small coastal resort town, is an excellent starting point for energetic walks as it is surrounded by woodlands, mountain scenery and seascapes. There's a long, safe open stretch of sand and visiting yachtsmen are welcome at the Sailing Club. There are opportunities for angling, riding, windsurfing or to play a round of golf on the town's nine-hole course.

Llandudno North Shore and Llanfairfechan are *Tidy Britain Seaside Award Winners*.

AT A GLANCE

Angling — Sea fishing from the pier all year round. Day tickets available at the pier. Tel: (01492) 876258.

Bait — Available from Kiosk by the Pier or from 'Llandudno Fishing Tackle', Craig-y-Don. Tel: (01492) 878425.

Boat Trips — Half-hour trips around Great Orme's Head depart frequently from the jetty, North Shore Promenade, May–September. Tel: (01492) 877394.

Fishing Trips — Organised by boatmen at Conwy and Llandudno. Contact the Harbour Master for further details. Tel: (01492) 596253.

GradeStudio

Here are two student responses to the exam question below about the leaflet trying to attract visitors to the seaside resort of Llandudno. Read the leaflet on page 47, and then read the answers together with the examiner comments. Then check what you have learnt and try putting it into practice.

Who is this leaflet trying to attract to Llandudno? (10 marks)

Read the leaflet on page 47

GradeStudio

Examiner tip

Remember that this question is asking 'who' the leaflet is trying to attract. It is not asking 'how' it attracts.

MAKE THE GRADE

D grade answer

Student 1

This leaflet is trying to attract everyone to Llandudno. They do this by having lots of different range of activities for everyone, so they give the impression that anyone and everyone would like it there. The pictures are bright and colourful, so this makes the leaflet eye catching to people looking for a place of fun and excitement. They include pictures of the beach, donkeys and views of Llandudno from afar, pictures of buildings that are structurally beautiful and children watching a Punch and Judy show. They use emotive and persuasive language. They tell us lots of information about such attraction in great detail with lots of persuasive language. It gives us lots of ways to get in contact with different places to help us and addresses and phone numbers of places we might like to visit.

Examiner comment

It is not true that the leaflet is trying to attract everyone. However, this answer gets the basic point that the leaflet is trying to attract a wide range of people by mentioning lots of different activities. It is true that the leaflet is attempting to attract people who like fun and excitement, although it is not really the colour of the pictures which does this. The answer lists a range of attractions but then drifts into vague comments about 'emotive' and 'persuasive' language. The last sentence of the answer is irrelevant and the answer loses focus on the question. This answer is at the top of grade D.

C grade answer

Student 2

The leaflet is trying to attract families to Llandudno. It mentions the attractions of 'paddling in the waters' and 'playing on the sands' which would appeal to families with young children. It also mentions 'Punch and Judy' and donkey rides and organised games. There are supervised activities for children which would appeal to parents. It says toddlers 'love' splashing about in the paddling pool. The pictures show a busy seaside with lots of children enjoying themselves. It also shows that Llandudno has won a 'Tidy Britain Seaside Award'. Yachtsmen are 'welcome' and anglers and riders are also attracted.

Examiner comment

This answer identifies families as the main target and produces some appropriate evidence to support that view. The answer picks out some of the activities which would appeal to families, particularly those with children, and there is some mention of the pictures. Other groups of people are only mentioned briefly but this answer is focused and, as far as it goes, it is sensible and clear. It just makes grade C.

Targeting an audience: how to go up the grades

To move up the grades these answers need to identify more of the specific groups of people who are being targeted by the leaflet. For example, the sea and sand are obviously attracting families with young children and the pictures of donkey rides and Punch and Judy reinforce that message.

There are other details such as Professor Peabody's Playplace and the paddling pool which would attract families with young children.

Older people might be attracted by the 'fun' activities and the possibility of sitting near the bandstand to listen to a 'visiting band'. Outdoor types might like the 'energetic walks' or the yachting, windsurfing, golf and fishing. The Cistercian monastery could attract anyone interested in history. The 'wonderful views' would attract those who visit for sightseeing and people who enjoy nature and perhaps some peace and quiet.

However, there is very little here which would appeal to most teenagers. They are not the target audience and so it is not really true that the leaflet appeals to 'everyone'.

There is no time to get distracted by colour or irrelevant details and you must avoid vague, and in this case irrelevant, comments about 'emotive' or 'persuasive' language.

Putting it into practice

On your own or with a partner, explain what you now know about:
- identifying the target audience of a text
- supporting your ideas by reference to the facts given in the text
- supporting your ideas by selecting and analysing key words and phrases.

In the future

- You must practise this type of question using a range of texts.
- Always start by asking yourself 'what kind of people does that appeal to?'
- Use details and words/phrases to support your answer.
- Make sure you include at least five or six types of people.
- Aim to produce a complete answer in 10–15 minutes.

GradeStudio

Examiner tip

Remember that you may not be the target audience. You need to think about other people and their interests. Be very careful about claiming that any text is aimed at 'everyone'.

My learning objectives ▼

- to practise questions about 'intended audience'
- to develop a clear understanding of what is required by this type of question.

Activity 1

Below is an 'intended audience' question. Read the leaflet on Blackpool Zoo below and answer the following question.

Who is this leaflet trying to attract to Blackpool Zoo? (10 marks)

EXHIBITIONS · AMPLE PARKING · MINIATURE RAILWAY · ANIMAL FEEDS · DINOSAURS

more than just a zoo...

Blackpool Zoo really is a day out for all the family. As well as the amazing animals, there is so much more to do, including browsing in our quality gift shops, dining in our family restaurant, or even enjoying a ride on our miniature railway. A coffee shop, exhibition area and conference room are located in the entrance area, and displays and theatre take place in our outdoor arena.

take a **closer** look!

education, conservation
family fun

FAMILY RESTAURANT · PLAY ZONE · LAKE & PARKLAND SETTING · GIFT SHOPS

GradeStudio

Examiner tips

- You should spend no more than 13–14 minutes on this question.
- Remember that you must identify the specific audiences.
- Be careful not to rush into claiming that leaflets attract 'everyone'.
- Each audience should be clearly linked to evidence from the text.

Peer/Self-assessment

1 Check your answers to Activity 1.
  - Did you find a range of target audiences?
  - Did you work through all of the text?
  - Did you find evidence in the text to support each of your comments?
  - Did you find any examples of particular words and phrases used by the writer to appeal to certain people?

2 Now try to grade your answer to Activity 1 using the mark scheme below. You will need to be careful and precise in your marking. Give a tick for each clear 'audience' and a tick for each piece of relevant evidence. The ticks will guide you to the correct mark, but you also need to make a judgement about the quality and coherence of the answer.

⬆ Moving up the grades

A   8–10 marks
- explores appropriate detail from the text with depth and insight
- best answers are thorough and perceptive, covering a range of points accurately and with an assured grasp of the intended audience.

C   5–7 marks
- selects appropriate detail from the text to show understanding of the intended audience
- better answers sustain a valid interpretation
- the answer has a clear focus on the question.

D   2–4 marks
- makes simple comments based on surface features of the text
- identifies some obvious targets
- some focus on the question.

GORILLA MOUNTAIN · AWARD-WINNING · LEMUR WOOD

meet the animals

Discover the secrets about our animals that only the keepers know! Our fantastic education team work alongside them to bring you a full programme of exciting talks and feeds throughout the day.

Blackpool Zoo is a great supporter of conservation projects around the world in many endangered habitats.

award-winning animal park

Elephants, gorillas, lions, tigers, orang utans, to name but a few – these are just some of the 400 species of mammals, birds, reptiles and invertebrates living here at Blackpool Zoo in 32 acres of stunning parkland and picturesque lakes. Safe, open spaces, play areas and natural enclosures invite visitors of all ages to enjoy their day at Blackpool Zoo.

ANIMAL DISPLAYS · THEATRE

Persuasive techniques

Persuasive writers can use a variety of techniques to attempt to influence an audience, and the exam questions will almost certainly require analysis of how a particular text does this. It could be selling a product or promoting an idea or a point of view, but writing is never really neutral, particularly this kind of writing.

As you read each text, try to establish a sense not only of its topic (what it is about) but also the writer's viewpoint (what the writer really thinks about the topic).

The questions are likely to be worded as follows:

▶ How does the writer try to encourage or interest or argue?

▶ How does this text try to persuade or attract or sell or influence?

You should consider the following points as you work through:

▶ approach	▶ tone
▶ content	▶ headlines and titles
▶ structure	▶ pictures
▶ language	▶ presentation.

You could learn the above checklist for the exam. Read the extract on the opposite page along with the annotations which show how these persuasive techniques work in practice. We will then look at each of them in turn through this section.

GradeStudio

Examiner tips

- The best way to proceed is to 'track' the text, taking each paragraph or section in turn. Most importantly, ask yourself: 'What is the intention behind this detail?', 'What is the effect?'
- This type of exam question is asking you to analyse how a writer tries to persuade. It is **not** asking whether you agree. You must look at what the writer is doing and not start giving your own views on the issue.
- The question is **not**: 'How does the writer make you want to read on?' So don't answer that question instead of the actual question!

GradeStudio

Examiner tips

Notice that it is not always possible, or necessary, to comment on every aspect of persuasive technique.
For example, there is no headline in the extract (opposite) and nothing really to say about presentation. Don't worry though, there is still a lot to say, as you can see.

Activity 1

The extract opposite by Fabienne Williams is about a racing driver called Katherine Legge. The annotations are in response to the following question:

How does the writer try to show the reader that Katherine Legge is a serious and talented racing driver? (10 marks)

Use the annotated text to produce an answer to this question in no more than fifteen minutes.

Few people outside the United States have seen Katherine Legge race. But plenty have seen her crash. YouTube has recorded more than 12,000 downloads of the clip of her accident in the 2006 Road America race, which shows her car
5 – travelling at 180mph – launching into the air, landing upside down and disintegrating against a wall in a cloud of smoke. Legge escaped with only bruised knees. 'I honestly thought I was going to be seriously injured,' she told me when we met at Daytona International Speedway in Florida, where she was
10 preparing for the track's famous 24-hour endurance race.

At 26, Legge, who is now partly based in Indiana, is one of the best racing drivers in the world, yet remains comparatively unknown at home in Britain. She races in the Champ Car World Series in high-performance single-seaters
15 that are the American equivalent of Formula One cars.
In 2005 she became the first woman to win a race in the Champ Car feeder series.

She was part of the karting scene that included current F1 drivers Jenson Button, Anthony Davidson and Lewis Hamilton –
20 and she has raced against all of them. Her childhood ambition was to be an F1 driver, an ambition that remains unchanged today. 'I'm stubborn and I won't be beaten by anything,' she says. […]

Legge is not chasing publicity and has refused every offer of
25 a glamour photoshoot […] .

'You get a lot of media attention in this sport as a girl because of the novelty factor,' she says, 'but where I'm trying to get to, that would lose you respect.'

Begins by admitting that not many people outside the USA have seen her race.

Then uses figures to show that many people have watched her in action.

Uses figures to show how fast she drives.

Uses dramatic and vivid language to show the risks she takes.

Uses interviews and quotations from Katherine Legge.

The race she is entering is 'famous' and a test of 'endurance'.

Uses the superlative to show she is 'one of the best'.

The cars are 'high performance' and the 'equivalent of Formula 1'.

She is the first woman to win a race.

She has competed against the best male drivers (Jenson Button and Lewis Hamilton).

Use of quotation to stress her ambition and determination (she admits she is 'stubborn').

Uses the example of refusing 'glamour' photographs to prove she is serious about her racing.

Use of quotation to emphasise she wants 'respect' as a driver.

The picture shows her in her racing leathers enjoying a moment of triumph.

My learning objectives ▼
- to understand how an underlying approach influences the reader
- to gain an overview of persuasive tactics.

Persuasive approaches

Putting forward an argument

To analyse persuasive writing you need to think about the underlying approach being used and how the writer tries to influence the reader. This is your opportunity to 'stand back' and analyse the bigger picture. Sometimes this is called 'overview', and it is really about the tactics a persuasive writer uses to put across an argument. For example, arguments can be won by:

- ▶ Pointing out the benefits or advantages, or what is to be gained (the positive case):
  - ▷ for the individual (you in particular)
  - ▷ for others
  - ▷ for society
  - ▷ for the environment.
- ▶ Pointing out the dangers or disadvantages or what could be lost, or attacking your opponents (the negative case):
  - ▷ for the individual
  - ▷ for others
  - ▷ for society
  - ▷ for the environment.

An argument in persuasive writing may focus on personal, social, environmental or moral issues. It may appeal to self-interest or our social or moral concerns. It may appeal to our better nature, give clear instructions, or use commands or orders (imperatives) politely!

Techniques to gain emotional responses are common features of persuasive writing. They can include:

- ▶ scare tactics (playing on your fears or insecurities)
- ▶ shock tactics (often sensational or creating outrage)
- ▶ an appeal to your hopes, dreams or ambitions
- ▶ an appeal to your vanity or snobbery
- ▶ an appeal to your better nature or idealism
- ▶ an appeal to your self-image.

GradeStudio

Examiner tips

- An argument can be put 'positively' but it can be 'negative' in undermining or contradicting the opposition. Often, persuasive writing will combine these two approaches: try to think about the 'underlying tactic' beneath the surface detail.
- Sometimes a writer will use personal or first-hand experience to give weight to what s/he is saying. Interviews and quotations may be important.

1   Read the extract below, then list the 'tactics', e.g. shock tactics
     (see the list opposite) that this writer uses.

2   For each tactic in your list, include at least one piece of evidence.

FOOD FOR THOUGHT – ARE WE A NATION OF FATTIES?

What did your children have for lunch today? Ask them. Go on. Actually, you don't have to bother. I can tell you. Chips were probably involved, a fizzy drink of some
5   sort, a greaseburger or some other deep-fried delicacy. This is, of course, a huge generalisation, and to those who do go for salad or spaghetti bolognese, I apologise. However, the sad fact is that we have bad
10 eating habits because that's what we've always known. We eat fatty, fried foods in school and it sets the pattern for later life. We need to change this, but how?

How many of you have been to a fast-food
15 restaurant this week? Come on, don't be shy. Too many are doing this in Britain. There's no excuse for it. It's not the cheapest option, and I'm prepared to bet it's not the tastiest either. We all know the risks, but we shrug our shoulders and carry on our path of artery-clogging
20 destruction. Why not go to a healthier food store? Heck, bring your own sandwiches, but don't do this to yourselves, people! Some of you reading this article, right now, could die as a result of your eating habits. Stop now. Cease this madness!
25 The McDonalds salads are your enemies too. They're just as fattening so don't be fooled by the marketing ploy. We all know what's healthy and what's not, so let's do something about it.

Persuasive content

Content is an important feature of any text. Almost all questions will focus on content to some extent, even the 'how' questions. Think about:

▶ **facts and opinions** (what is said, the selection of material, the points writers choose to suit their purpose)

▶ the **arguments used by the writer**

▶ the use of **examples**

▶ the use of **statistics or figures**

▶ the use of **quotations** (often from experts or personalities such as Lewis Hamilton or Jamie Oliver to give 'celebrity endorsement' and encourage others to follow their example).

When you are answering a question about persuasive techniques identify the features that you think have an effect and consider why they are there and exactly what effect they achieve. Find and mention the underlying techniques, but always back them up with specific examples from the text and explain what effect they have.

Activity 1

1 The article opposite was written by a teenage girl in response to the representation of teenagers by the comedian Harry Enfield who created the character 'Kevin the Teenager'. Read the article and answer the question below.

How does the writer try to suggest that parents are as bad as teenagers? (10 marks)

2 Read through some of the points that you could use to answer this question:

● she gives examples of the way her mother behaves like a stereotypical teenager (the rolling eyes, the sighs, the lack of explanation, hiding away in her room, slamming doors, answering back and making sarcastic comments)

● she adopts a sarcastic tone and presents her mother as a parody of the typical teenager ('we wouldn't understand')

● she accuses her mother of being a hypocrite (the alcohol, chocolate and money) and motivated by guilt as 'she knows that is how she should behave'

● she claims her mother has far worse moods than she does and overreacts to trivial problems (she gets 'obsessed' with 'stupid stuff' like a discarded towel while an uncleaned bath becomes 'the end of the world')

● she says she is as self-absorbed and immature as any teenager (she can be irritable for a whole day about her 'problems')

● Dad is just as hypocritical (the TV)

● she gives examples of her mother spending money on self-indulgent luxuries (flowers, wine, silk pyjamas)

● she says they are as untidy as she is (her dad piles his clothes on a chair in the bedroom).

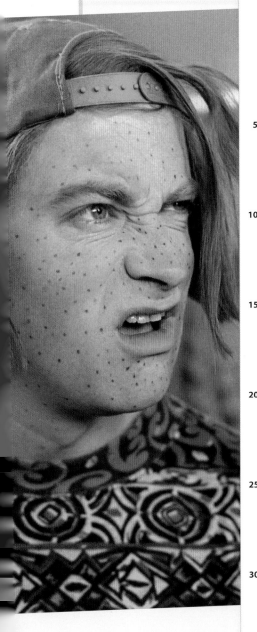

WHO'S THE REAL KEVIN?

Harry Enfield's Kevin is the 'typical' teenager: grumpy, moody, awkward and sulky. But in our house he is definitely more
5 like my mother than me.

One of her specialities is that most stereotypical of teenage habits – rolling her eyes and sighing. She won't tell us why of
10 course – we wouldn't understand. Instead she disappears to her study and starts thumping away at her word processor. She's also just as likely to slam doors,
15 answer back or make biting, sarcastic comments.

Another thing that teenagers are always told off for is hypocrisy. The words 'double standards' are
20 constantly ringing in my ears. My Mum tells us that we shouldn't drink alcohol/eat chocolate/ spend too much money because she knows that is how she should
25 behave. However, her nagging would be more effective if she wasn't telling us this in our new, ridiculously expensive kitchen, while drinking white wine and
30 munching chocolate.

Mum has far worse moods than I do. She'll suddenly get obsessed about stupid stuff, such as us leaving towels on the bathroom
35 floor and not cleaning the bath. She behaves as if it's the end of the world. At other times she'll get annoyed when I start doing my homework late on Sunday
40 nights – as if she's the one to get detention if I don't finish it on time. It's ridiculous to trust me to be responsible enough to ride on public transport on my own, and not think I can organise my
45 own schoolwork. I understand that she worries about me but she can be irritable for a whole day – about not being able to work the video, about her work not going
50 well, about the sausages burning or that nothing in her wardrobe fits her.

My Dad is just as guilty. We are told off daily for watching too
55 much cable TV, as are most of my friends. And yet my Dad is having a giant plasma screen installed (with satellite box of course) so he can spend hours on Sunday watching
60 his football team lose. Again.

My parents are very typical when it comes to money. I'm nagged about spending too much money on magazines, and yet
65 Mum spends more than double my allowance on flowers, wine and silk pyjamas – she has five pairs. Untidiness, however, must be the worst sin. My room is,
70 usually, untidy. I don't deny it and neither do most teenagers I know. Yet my parents can't see that their bedroom is untidy too. Almost every item of my Dad's clothing is
75 piled on to a chair in the corner of their room.

In my view, teenagers get a very unfair representation in the papers and on TV. My parents can be just
80 as bad as me. In fact, I should ring Harry Enfield. I have loads of material for two new characters.

GradeStudio

Here are two student responses to the exam question below about the article 'Who's the real Kevin?' on page 57. Read the answers together with the examiner comments, then check what you have learnt and try putting it into practice.

How does the writer try to suggest that parents are as bad as teenagers? (10 marks)

C grade answer

Student 1

The way the writer tries to suggest that parents are as bad as teenagers is what she tells us about the activity parents are involved in which sometimes we get the stick for. She tells us parents get into just as many moods, tantrums, disagreements and arguments as us teenagers do. ✓ Another thing she brings up is they tell us not to 'spend loads of money' or 'eat chocolate or drink wine' while she's there in her new kitchen drinking white wine and eating chocolate. ✓ It's like they are trying to bully us around and they can carry on with what they like. The way she expresses this is she tries to say it like they are just a bunch of idiots and they waste their time for eg 'watching his team on the plasma, losing. Again!' As if he has no clue in anything. They try to make us think they cannot trust us when it's them we can't trust. She makes out they are hypocrites. ✓ She then tries to mock her parents' childish ways ✓ by saying she should ring Harry Enfield and tell him how she has loads of material for two new characters. ✓

General but some grasp.

So clumsy that the meaning is unclear.

Misses the obvious inference but the detail is relevant.

Losing focus on the question.

Examiner comment

This answer struggles for total clarity in thought and expression but there are some valid points. The focus is not secure and it is lacks some detail; but it just does enough to get to grade C.

Student 2

The writer starts off by introducing the 'typical' teenager as 'Kevin' but she immediately makes it clear that she feels that this is an inaccurate representation. In fact, her mother has more 'Kevin' traits than her. ✓ Mother is the one who rolls her eyes and sighs like a moody teenager. ✓ She goes on to examine these stereotypes and compare them to her parents' behaviour. First, she describes her mother's sulkiness and mood swings. ✓ For example, 'slamming doors' or 'thumping' at her computer. ✓ Another example of her juvenile behaviour is, apparently, her tendency to get wound up over trivial matters, 'stupid stuff' such as towels on the bathroom floor. ✓ She also highlights the hypocrisy of both of her parents. ✓ Her mother tells her not to eat chocolate or drink alcohol but does so while munching chocolate and drinking a glass of wine. ✓ She also mentions their self-indulgence. ✓ Her mother has five pairs of silk pyjamas while her father spends money on a plasma television but tells her not to watch too much. ✓ She regards this with utmost derision. ✓ She sees the 'untidiness' of her parents as a cardinal sin despite their continual 'nagging' at her to clean her bedroom. ✓

Inferences clearly made

Inferences clearly made

Examiner comment

This answer starts a little uncomfortably but then shows good understanding and never loses sight of the question. There are clear inferences here such as the hypocrisy and self-indulgence of her parents and also an assured selection of textual detail to give substance to the answer. It is mostly 'what she says' that makes the writer's case and this answer unpicks the material very well indeed. It would achieve a grade A*.

How to go up the grades

To move up the grades you need to focus on the question but, above all, you need to stay close to the text and select and use relevant details. Some of these will certainly be content, some will almost certainly be language and there may be other techniques which you can identify and try to analyse.

Try to develop your skill in using short quotations and weaving them into your answer. Make sure that you read all of the specified lines.

Follow the sequence of the text and take the relevant points as you find them.

Putting it into practice

On your own or with a partner explain what you now know about:

- identifying the persuasive techniques in a text
- supporting your ideas by reference to the content of the text
- supporting your ideas by selecting and analysing key words and phrases
- identifying other techniques used to persuade
- what makes the difference between a grade C answer and a grade A* answer.

In the future

- You must practise this type of question using a range of texts.
- Use details and words/phrases to support your answer.
- Make sure you give specific examples of any techniques you identify.
- Always work methodically through the text.
- Aim to produce a complete answer in 10–15 minutes.

My learning objectives ▼
- to understand what is meant by the structure of a text
- to understand how writers use structure to influence readers.

Persuasive structure

Structure is how a text is organised or put together. Writers make choices about what to include but they also make choices about the order in which they present an argument. Sometimes it is important to look at the steps in an argument to see the underlying structure. You are really just looking at the order in which the content of the text has been assembled.

Activity 1

1 Read the Oxfam advertisement opposite. It is obviously emotional and was intended to influence readers into helping to end poverty by giving money every month. The content and language are powerful and the tone is conversational and polite, trying to engage the reader directly as an individual and tug at the heartstrings.

2 Now read the corresponding numbered comments below about how the argument is structured. The way the text is put together helps Oxfam to get its message across.

3 Having learnt how the Oxfam piece is put together, remind yourself of 'Who's the real Kevin?' on page 57. Identify the steps of the argument that the writer uses in her article. You could use bullet points to do this.

GradeStudio

Examiner tip

MAKE THE GRADE ✔ MAKE THE GRADE

If you follow the structure of a text, identifying the 'steps' in the argument, you can look for other features as you go. For example, at the end of the appeal from Oxfam you could pick up the polite use of 'please' as an example of how tone is used to appeal to our better nature.

How the Oxfam advert is structured

1 The headline establishes a personal, individual viewpoint and claims that the person is 'in' because the money given is clearly, and visibly, 'saving lives'.

2 Oxfam then gives specific examples of how we are lucky. For example, it reminds us that we have enough to eat and drink and our children get an education. It also suggests that we have money to spend on luxuries and entertainment such as CDs.

3 The text then contrasts our comfortable lifestyle with the 'extreme poverty' endured by 'millions' of people around the world.

4 Oxfam then makes it clear that the £8 which we might spend on something like a CD could be the difference between life and death.

5 The next move is to claim that 'you' can help to end poverty by saying 'I'm in'. It insists that poverty is a 'moral injustice' and gives a number of ways in which we can help.

6 It lists what can be achieved by relatively small amounts of money, using bullet points to get the message across clearly and simply.

7 It tries to show that progress has been made and quotes a specific example in Zambia. It wants us to feel that we really can make a difference.

8 The advert ends with an appeal and clear directions about how to get involved.

9 The picture shows an individual, an 'ordinary' person, who is prepared to give money. She illustrates that it is just people like us who donate money to Oxfam, although her gender and ethnicity may be significant.

I can see my money saving lives. That's why 'I'm in'

We're pretty lucky, aren't we? Our children will get an education. We have plenty to eat and drink. And that £8 in our pocket? Well, we'll probably use it to buy a CD or something.

But for millions of people living in extreme poverty around the world, it's a very different story. That £8, for example, could be the difference between living and dying. You can help end poverty by saying 'I'm in'.

What it means to say 'I'm in'.

Saying 'I'm in' is a powerful statement. It means you've chosen to join a movement of people who believe that poverty is a moral injustice and can be overcome. You can give money, volunteer your time, campaign for change, put pressure on world leaders, or simply offer your name as a sign of support. Being 'in' is your way of saying enough is enough to poverty. Right now, we're asking for money. Whatever suits your wallet. Let's see what your monthly gift could achieve:

- **£8 could buy a mosquito net, which protects a family from malaria.**
- **£18 could provide safe drinking water for 25 people.**
- **£30 could build a toilet, which prevents the spread of diseases like cholera and diarrhoea.**
- **£46 could train a midwife, to safely deliver babies.**

Progress is being made. Be part of it.

The past year has seen real improvements. In April this year, for example, the government of Zambia introduced free health care for people living in rural areas. Those who couldn't afford medical help can now come forward for vital treatment. It happened because of people giving their voices in support of ending poverty. We'd like you to build on this success by saying 'I'm in'.

Please give what you can.

It's your way of saying 'I'm in'. Complete and return the attached form or call 0870 410 5025.

Visit www.oxfam.org.uk/in

Language used to influence

The selection of content is part of a writer's technique, but it is important to look at the use of language too. This involves not just finding key words and phrases, but also thinking about their purpose and effect.

GradeStudio

MAKE THE GRADE ✓

Examiner tip

When you identify words or phrases which you think are significant and relevant, always ask yourself 'what is the word or phrase showing or suggesting to the reader?' This will help you to push on and try to comment on the use of language.

Activity 1

1 Read the extract opposite, from an article about a boxing match in which a young fighter called Spencer Oliver was badly injured.

2 You would certainly have things to say about the content of this writing, but language is also important in creating the sense of horror.

The impressions the reader gets from this article are:
- Oliver is taking a lot of punches
- the punches are very powerful
- they are having a dreadful impact on him.

a Which word in the first sentence suggests that things were not looking good for Oliver?

b What is the effect of the writer using the phrase 'within seconds' in the first sentence?

c Look at the second sentence. Pick out three words from this sentence which you would include in your answer. What is the effect of these words?

d What does the verb 'hauled' tell you about Oliver's physical condition?

e Which other two words in that sentence show you that Oliver was in serious trouble?

f What does the phrase 'rained in blows' tell you about what was happening to Oliver?

g Pick out two more words from that paragraph which show the power of the punches and the effect they were having.

h Look at the final two paragraphs and make a list of the words you would want to include in your answer.

3 Time is short in exams, so pick out **four** words from the whole extract that you think are particularly effective.

Daily Mail

What can be said now in defence of this sport?

Within seconds of Oliver's triumphal ring entrance, the signs were catastrophic.

Oliver was decked with a wild hook which caught him flush on the chin. He hauled
5 himself off the canvas but looked groggy and spent. Referee Alfred Azaro looked into his eyes and allowed the fight to continue.

The 3000 crowd in the half-full Royal Albert Hall tried to raise Oliver's spirits by
10 continually chanting his name.

Many of these knowledgeable fans would have witnessed the chill which went through the London Arena three years ago during Nigel Benn's fight with the American Gerald
15 McClellan.

In an awful twist, the referee on that terrible night was also Azaro, who stood in the ring aghast as McClellan was stretchered out and ended up with permanent brain
20 damage.

Oliver tried to respond, but Devakov rained in blows which the usually fleet-of-foot Oliver failed to dodge. Devakov stunned him […] with a punishing shot to
25 the temple.

As the tenth round began, Oliver looked weak and drained. The warning signs were there, and when a stunning right hook exploded onto his chin the audience rose in
30 shock.

Oliver, his gumshield dropping to the floor, looked up at referee Azaro with an expression which was utterly terrible. It was that of a scared young child seeking
35 solace. He held out his hands pleading for help and then fell in a crumple to the canvas. […] The crowd watched in horror as he lay unconscious in the ring.

Read the extract below, written by a girl who read the article on page 63 about Spencer Oliver and wanted to express her opinions about the sport of boxing.

I would like to begin by saying that I am vehemently opposed to boxing. I find that it is a barbaric sport, glorifying violence and blood with little moral or social justification.

The supporters of boxing would say that boxing spectators are merely fans of
5 sport, and that they enjoy the art and technique in the sport. I am afraid that I disagree with this claim. A boxing audience's main interest is in the gratuitous violence and testosterone-fuelled machismo which compels one man to hit another.

Another reason that would be cited in defence of boxing is the help which it gives to those who are socially disadvantaged. They would say that boxing gives them respect
10 and turns them into honest citizens. One only needs to look at the case of Mike Tyson, a convicted rapist who is, nevertheless a famous boxer and therefore is welcomed with open arms into this country, to see the stupidity of that. The law is that people convicted of serious crimes are not allowed into Britain. Mike Tyson has been in prison for committing the crime of rape – an abhorrent crime, and yet because he
15 is famous and may generate some prosperity for the financial backers of boxing he is welcomed without a qualm. Not just once, though that in itself was despicable enough, but twice, therefore proving that cash and not conscience rules the world today.

As well as this unfairness there is the large body of evidence supporting the fact that boxing is a dangerous sport. How many people have to have permanent
20 brain damage or die before the government comes to its senses. As an example there is the recent case of Spencer Oliver, a young boxer who was carried out on a stretcher after a fight and is still in danger in a hospital. What about the countless others, dead or as good as dead, who have been cut down? We have laws prohibiting the fighting of dogs or cock-fighting, and yet we have so little regard to
25 our fellow-men that we continue to allow this blood-thirsty, cruel sport. There may be medical officers on hand at all times during a boxing match, but what use is that when one blow could be enough to sever the life-thread of a young boxer?

I would like to conclude by making this point: we cannot continue to hide behind the fact that illegal boxing is dangerous, when it is blatantly obvious that legalised
30 boxing is not only dangerous, but damaging, demeaning, and ultimately spells death for the participant, while the sport's promoters and managers earn unholy amounts of money, with little or no risk to themselves.

This writer is strongly opposed to the sport of boxing and uses a variety of techniques to make her case. However, she does not actually have many facts at her disposal and she relies quite heavily on her use of language to persuade her readers.

Activity 2

Answer the following questions which focus on the language used in the extract opposite.

1. The first paragraph makes it clear that the writer is opposed to boxing. Which word makes it clear that her feelings are very strong?

2. She uses the word 'barbaric' to describe the sport. What is the effect of using this word?

3. She claims that boxing 'glorifies' violence and blood. What does she mean when she adds that it has 'little moral or social justification'?

4. In the second paragraph the writer attacks the supporters of boxing and tries to undermine the claim that its fans simply enjoy the 'art and technique' of the fighters. Which word does she use to suggest that the violence is uncalled for?

5. The writer describes the boxers as 'testosterone-fuelled'. What impression of the boxers does this create in your mind?

6. The next paragraph uses the example of Mike Tyson, who was a world champion but also a convicted rapist. Find two words in this paragraph which show the writer's strong disapproval of his crime.

7. The writer then uses the example of Spencer Oliver. She is rather emotional when she discusses his injuries and the damage done to 'countless others'. Pick out two adjectives which you could use to show her disgust at boxing.

8. It is always sensible to use short quotations, and it is even better when you can select individual words on which you can comment. Which single word in the final paragraph shows this writer's attitude to the people who run the sport of boxing?

GradeStudio

Examiner tip

Don't use 'chunks' of text. Try to limit your use of quotations to a few words. Single words or short phrases work best and you can use your own words to link them together and comment on the effect of language.

MAKE THE GRADE

Persuasive tone

Tone

Tone is the way something is said or written, or the manner in which the reader is addressed. Writers adopt various tones, just as we do in speech, depending on whom they are addressing and what they are trying to achieve. Most of us learn at an early age how to use tone to try to get what we want!

Think about the question 'Please can I have…?' How exactly would you say this? Your answer means that you are beginning to understand tone.

Similarly, if you fall off your chair in class, the teacher may say: 'Well, that was clever.' The meaning is the exact opposite of the literal meaning of the words. The sarcasm is achieved through tone.

When you are reading, think about the tone the writer adopts and the reason for it. There is a contrast between texts that want to seem factual and reasonable and those that are expressing strong feelings. Writers may take the emotional heat out of an issue (usually if they writing a defensive piece). Others may seek as much emotional impact as possible. Occasionally, these can be fiercely one-sided, making no attempt to be balanced.

Activity 1

How many words can you think of to describe a writer's tone?
Below are some words you could use to describe a writer's tone.
You could learn some of these so that you have a bank of words to use in the exam.
Use a dictionary to check the meaning of any words you do not know.

calm	aggressive	formal	ranting
serious	ironic/sarcastic	reasonable	emotional
factual	opinionated	conversational/colloquial	informal
measured	elevated	flippant/lighthearted	earnest

Activity 2

Read the three extracts on the opposite page.
1 Which words from the list above best describe the tone of these articles?
2 For each article, write down the examples that made you choose the description of the tone.

Activity 3

Try to write a sentence commenting on how the tone of the articles is created by the examples you have found.

Extract 1

I took a train to Liverpool. They were having a festival of litter when I arrived.
Citizens had taken time off from their busy activities to add crisp packets, empty
cigarette boxes, and carrier-bags to the otherwise bland and neglected landscape.
They fluttered gaily in the bushes and brought colour and texture to pavements
5 and gutters. And to think that elsewhere we stick these objects in rubbish bags.

Extract 2

When somebody mentions the word exercise, your brain immediately switches off. It has all sorts of nasty connotations; sweaty gym shorts, dry mouth, aching lungs. You probably 5 remember past PE lessons – endless laps around a muddy field or hockey in the freezing cold and driving rain.

Well, surprisingly, exercise does not have to be this way. It can be enjoyable and it doesn't 10 even have to hurt. You don't even have to leave the comfort of your own home. Intrigued? Well, you should be.

Many people nowadays are choosing to do non-cardiovascular exercises, like yoga, or pilates. Non-cardiovascular is a big word, but all 15 it really means is that you don't have to end up panting and clutching a stitch.

Exercises like yoga still work your muscles, but they don't put a lot of strain on your heart and lungs. You still get many of the benefits of 20 going for a run. Your muscles become toned and fat can be burned, but just with less effort.

Extract 3

Lowestoft is the most easterly point on the British Isles. It is also, I would add, one of
the most ugly. The faint odour of Thatcherite depression surrounds the town, with its
outskirts of abandoned factories and its centre of cheap burger joints and toyshops.

For all those people who wish to have their romantic image of Suffolk – rolling fields,
5 country ale and slightly simple locals – shattered, Lowestoft is the place to go.

It is, inevitably, a grey day, as you drive along the road running parallel to the pier.
The sea and the sky have seemingly merged into a grey mass, yet the beach is packed
with holidaymakers showing all their 'Dunkirk spirit', as they resolutely continue their
holidays amidst the horrible conditions.

10 The seafront reeks of greasy fish and chips, the arcades are shut for restoration,
but the holidaymakers are smiling and enjoying themselves. No matter how horrible
the weather, people come to Lowestoft and enjoy themselves. Please excuse my faintly
incredulous tone, but there truly is something about Lowestoft that draws beach-addicts
like Glastonbury attracts middle-aged hippies.

Persuasive headlines and titles

All headlines and titles try to 'catch the eye' or 'grab the attention', but you need to go further than this in an exam answer. It is true that headlines are used to draw the reader in, but you must describe **how** a particular headline or title makes its impact. You should be making points that apply **only** to the **particular** headline you are referring to. You need to think about its intended effect on the reader. Ask: Why this headline? What is it achieving? How?

Headlines are often used to introduce a topic clearly, but sometimes they withhold information in an attempt to intrigue, or even mislead, the reader. Some common features of headlines and titles are:

▶ direct address (the use of 'you' to engage the reader as an individual)

▶ questions (sometimes rhetorical but often direct)

▶ sensational, dramatic or emotive language for impact

▶ play on words (often witty: puns, alliteration, rhyme etc.).

The headline below came from an advertisement from Friends of the Earth, who were campaigning against the trade in wood from the Amazon rainforest.

PLEASE WILL YOU STOP PAYING TO HAVE MY PEOPLE MURDERED?

Here are two examples of what students said about this headline:

Student 1

The advertisement uses emotive language to make you want to read on. It is a big, bold headline and uses a question which makes it effective.

Examiner comment

The problem here is that the comments are so vague. There is no attempt to identify the use of 'emotive language' and no attempt to say how it works. It is hard to imagine any headline that is not 'big and bold'. The headline does ask a question, but this answer just claims that it is 'very effective' without even trying to say how.

Student 2

> The headline confronts the reader by asking a direct question to make us feel involved and it is intriguing because the readers do not know how they are paying to have people 'murdered'. 'Murdered' is a very emotive word and the reader is meant to feel shocked and guilty and the word 'please' is like a plea to us to change our behaviour.

Examiner comment

This is much better; it focuses on the techniques and the specific words in the headline. It sees that the direct question is a way of 'confronting' readers and making it personal and it is true that readers would be asking how they are paying to have people murdered. The word 'murdered' is picked out but there is also a sensible comment which describes its effect. The comment on the use of 'please' is also good. The only way this answer could be improved would be to add something about the polite tone of the appeal: it is not aggressive, but it appeals to our better nature.

Activity 1

Now try to explain what the following headlines are about and why they are effective.

Doctor Who?

No light at the end of le tunnel

There's not mushroom in lunch boxes for healthy food

Ministers feel the heat at climate change summit

It's snow joke

Activity 2

Find a couple of headlines of your choice from a newspaper or magazine and write a short comment on each, saying what they contribute to the article and how effective they are.

GradeStudio

Examiner tip

Don't worry if you can't think of anything useful to say about a particular headline. If you do comment on it, say something specific and precise. You will get no marks for simply saying that a headline is 'big and bold and makes you want to read on'.

MAKE THE GRADE

My learning objective ▼

- to understand how pictures and presentation contribute to influencing readers.

Persuasive pictures and layout

Visual images convey obvious, and sometimes less obvious, messages. It is usually helpful to think about a picture in relation to the text it accompanies. A picture can illustrate and/or reinforce a message. It can give reality and individuality to someone or something.

A picture may be intended to shock, to attract, or to arouse emotion. Always try to analyse the intention and the effect of pictures in texts. You will get higher marks if you go further than simply describing what is in the picture. Some articles have more than one picture, and you should consider all of them in your response.

When looking at pictures, ask yourself:

▶ Why this picture? What is its effect?

▶ Is each picture giving the same message?

▶ Do the pictures work together to reinforce the message of the text?

▶ Do the pictures give different messages? If so, why?

Remember, a picture will usually link to the headline and the main text.

Activity 1

Look at the picture below, then answer the questions that follow.

1 Why this picture? What is its effect?
2 Does the picture reinforce the message of the headline? If so, how?
3 Does the picture give a different message from the headline? If so, how?

Save the planet – give up meat

Presentation

This is not usually a major or decisive factor in the persuasive impact of a text. Occasionally there is something useful to say, but don't get sidetracked. Look for:

▶ use of bold type or colour

▶ layout of text (bullets, fonts, text boxes)

▶ logos.

And always ask, 'What is the point or the effect of this?' For example, some techniques are used to highlight particular features and the purpose of a logo is to encourage 'recognition' and give credibility.

Activity 2

Working in pairs, identify as many of these logos as you can. For each one, answer the following questions.

1 What does the logo suggest to you?

2 Do you think it is an effective logo? Why/why not?

3 Why did the company or organisation choose this logo?

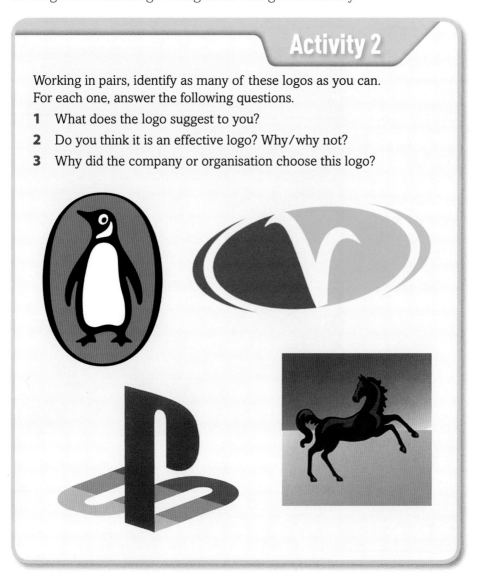

Comments on presentation should not dominate your answers. The appearance and presentation of a text may attract your attention or catch your interest, but that is only the first part of the job. The really important part is **persuading**. No one is likely to be persuaded by a text simply because of its layout.

Putting together the persuasive techniques

Now it's time to put together all that you have learnt about persuasive techniques. Read the following article.

The Guardian

Letters

Am I worth £30,000?

Am I worth £30,000? In my career I have been taught skills to save life, prolong life and to know when to walk away when there is no life left. I have taken courses to fight
5 fire from within, above and below. I can cut a car apart in minutes and I can educate your sons and daughters to save their own lives.

No matter what the emergency, I am part of a team that always comes when you call.
10 I run in when all my instincts tell me to run away. I have faced death in cars with petrol pouring over me while the engine was ticking with the heat. I have lain on my back inside a house fire and watched the
15 flames roar across the ceiling above me. I have climbed and I have crawled to save life and I have stood and wept while we buried a fellow firefighter.

I have been the target for yobs throwing
20 stones and punches at me while I do my job. I have been the first to intercept a parent who knows their son is in the car we are cutting up, and I know he is dead. I have served my time, damaged my body and seen
25 things that I hope you never will. I have never said 'No, I'm more important than them', and walked away.

Am I worth £30k? Maybe now your answer is no. But when that drunk smashes into your car, or the candle burns down too low,   30 or your child needs help, you will find I'm worth every last penny.

Jay Curson
Firefighter, Nottingham

The piece of paper below shows the notes a student made before writing an answer to the question:

How does the letter written to a newspaper by a fireman try to persuade you why his work is worth the £30,000 a year he is paid? (10 marks)

Approach	Emotional appeals to the reader
	Slang for dramatic effect
	Images to transcend time (e.g. 'candle burns down too low')
Content	Tells us he knows skills to save a life
	Tells us he knows skills to prolong life
	Tells us he knows how to fight fire from within, above and below
	Tells us he can cut a car open in minutes
	Tells us he can educate your sons and daughters to save their own lives
	Part of a team that always comes when you call
	Has stood and wept while a fellow firefighter was buried
	Been targeted by yobs who have thrown stones and punches while doing his job
	Never said 'I am more important than you' and walked away
Language	Repeated use of first person (I) and 'I have'
	Play on words 'run in ... run away'
Structure	Starts with a rhetorical question (e.g. 'am I worth £30,000?')
	Verbal patterning – repeats words within sentences and in related sentences
	Triplets (groups of three) used throughout
	Rhetorical question repeated later in the final paragraph
Tone	Use of cliché (e.g. 'seen things that I hope you never will')
	Ambiguous responses (e.g. 'served my time')
Headlines	Rhetorical question
Pictures	Close-up of fireman's face
	Emotive
Presentation	Four clear sections
	Sophisticated, accurate grammar (e.g. I have lain)
	Uses questions to make us think about the issues

Examiner tips

- 'How' is partly a matter of content/structure and partly a matter of language/tone. Other features may also be significant.
- Look for a clear sense of 'how' as opposed to simply 'what'. The best answers take the 'extra step' to *analyse* the detail rather than spotting it.

The planning in the notes on page 73 is very thorough. You are unlikely to produce this much in the 10–15 minutes you should spend answering this question in the exam. So, you need to be able to identify the key points that relate to the question:

How does the letter written to a newspaper by a fireman try to persuade you why his work is worth the £30,000 a year he is paid? (10 marks)

Activity 1

1   In pairs, using the notes on page 73 or your own ideas, write down the main points you think your answer should include.

2   On your own, in no more than 15 minutes, write an answer to the question above.

One of the problems that students have in answering this type of question is finding the right words, often the verbs, to allow them to say precisely what they mean. A range of vocabulary helps you avoid the monotonous repetition of 'the writer says…' You might find some of the following words useful as a way of introducing what you say when you analyse a writer's technique:

- describes
- mentions
- tells
- suggests
- shows
- insists
- compares
- gives (details/examples)
- emphasises
- uses (examples/facts/statistics/quotations/irony/humour/personal experience)

Peer/Self-assessment

Check your answers to Activity 1.

- Did you find a range of persuasive techniques?
- Did you work through all of the text?
- Did you use evidence in the text to support each of your comments?
- Did you find any examples of particular words and phrases used by the writer to appeal to certain people?
- How many of the items on the checklist did you decide to use?

Now try to grade your answer to Activity 1 using the mark scheme below. You will need to be careful and precise in your marking. Give a tick for each clear persuasive technique. The ticks will guide you to the correct mark but you also need to make a judgement about the quality and coherence of the answer.

Moving up the grades

A 8–10 marks
- explores the text in detail and with depth and insight
- the best answers are thorough and perceptive, covering a range of persuasive techniques accurately and with an assured grasp of 'how'.

C 5–7 marks
- selects appropriate detail from the text to make valid comments
- some spotting of key words/ phrases
- better answers clearly address the issue of 'how'
- better answers have a clear focus on the persuasive techniques.

D 2–4 marks
- makes simple comments based on surface features of text
- identifies some obvious persuasive techniques
- some evidence from the text is used.

GradeStudio

The start of Petronella Wyatt's article about riding the TT course in the Isle of Man can be found on page 39. Here is the rest of her article and two student responses to the exam question below.

How does Petronella Wyatt get across to you what it is like to ride the TT course? (10 marks)

Read the article, the answers and the examiner comments.

Daily Mail

THE FASTEST LADY ON TWO WHEELS!

Early the next morning, Simon introduces me to Milky. […] He is on the weedy side, with watery eyes and a pale face with a dreamy expression. […]

5 […] We go over and look at the bikes. They are monstrous. […]

Fortunately, I see a smaller, safer-looking machine in the corner that resembles more of a motorised bicycle. 10 'I'll ride that one,' I say.

'But that's a 1907 bike,' protests Simon. 'It only goes up to 25mph.'

'That's why I'll ride it.' Milky is having none of it […] and I am dragged 15 over to a gargantuan Suzuki 1000. Milky takes the bike over to the grandstand.

[…] I notice that the starting line is opposite a graveyard. This rather does for my composure […] but Milky is on 20 the bike, raring to go. […]

I put on my crash helmet and clamber onto the pillion seat […].

Milky is wearing straps around his waist, which I am supposed to hold on 25 to. […]

I am instructed to punch him if I become nervous. He has evidently never taken a course in logic. In order to punch him, I would have to let go of the straps. 30 If I let go of the straps I will fall off and break open my head.

It is, as the youth of today would say, a no-brainer. Unfortunately, that seems to be exactly what Milky is as well.

35 He revs up and we head towards a village on the north-east shore. Before us is a series of evil-looking bends.

Suddenly, Milky drops his elbow and opens the throttle. I am nearly thrown 40 over the front of the bike.

Ahead of us is Ballaugh Bridge. Ballaugh Bridge is no laughing matter. It has seen eight fatalities in three years. 'Stop going so fast,' I scream at Milky. 45 He accelerates. Then […] he decides to brake. My head flies forward as if it has been severed by an axe.

'I just thought I'd stop to point out areas of interest on the course,' Milky 50 explains. 'We are just about to approach Ballagarey Corner. It is one of the most dangerous on the village circuit.' He continues cheerfully, 'Once, I lost a mate there.'

55 'Lost him? You mean he took a wrong turning?'

'No, he crashed and went home in a coffin.'

We round the corner at 120mph. […] 60 Sweat is trickling down my arms. […]

Another graveyard flashes by. Does this island consist only of graveyards? Finally, we leave for the Snaefell Mountain Course. […]

65 Milky tells me we will get up to such speed that to any bystanders I will be a blur. I say I do not want to be a blur. I can see the obituary in the newspapers: 'A blur died yesterday while attempting 70 the Isle of Man TT course.'

But there is no reasoning with Milky, who is not only higher than a kite, but convinced I am his best ever pillion passenger […].

75 The mountain course dips and swerves […] and there are boulders and abysses everywhere.

I see a few sheep. I suppose if I have to land on anything, I would rather 80 it was a sheep. As Milky opens the throttle again, we hurtle past another unencouraging sign: 'Be very careful. 164 casualties in 3 years.'

We are on dangerous ground. In fact, 85 we are no longer on the ground at all. We are going so fast we are flying three feet above it. 'Where's the bloody ground gone?' I croak.

Scenery seems to have become 90 animate, zooming towards me. All at once we are back on the ground, but I don't like it any better, for my left ear is nearly scraping it. A passing lorry almost hits us. I think I am going to black out.

95 Then, suddenly, I feel a massive surge of adrenaline […]. It has finally happened […] and I want it to go on forever. But Milky slows down and finally brakes.

'How fast did we go?' I gasp. He 100 looks at me oddly. He tells me we have hit 166mph and have broken the course's pillion speed record.

[…] I shriek with primeval ecstasy. I insist we do a lap of triumph. As we 105 pass bemused pedestrians I punch the air and shout out […], 'Look at me. I'm on top of the world!'

Student 1

Sensible comments.

Clear sense of overview.

Apt quotations but not handled very elegantly.

Not quite the point but a reasonable attempt.

These could be helpful snippets of text but they are misused here.

Trying to look at techniques but doesn't know what to make of it.

It is not certain that Petronella is exaggerating.

Misses the point of what she is saying about the ride.

Clumsy and unclear.

Vaguely sees her change of feeling but no evidence.

Petronella Wyatt explains the ride as some kind of hellish ride. She makes it sound deadly and evil. 'I notice that the starting line is opposite a graveyard', 'a series of evil-looking bends'. Also, when Milky tells her his mate went home from there in a coffin, it makes the ride sound even more spooky and dangerous. Petronella exaggerates what happens throughout the article. 'My head flies forward as if it has been severed by an axe' and 'we are going so fast we are flying' are examples of her exaggeration to really express how amazing the ride was.

In the article, she puts speech in and most of what she says are questions to Milky which shows the reader how she felt unsure and nervous about what would happen next. 'Where's the bloody ground gone?' although seeming very scared through the whole ride, she tells us at the end that she wanted to do it again. In the last column she uses a few short sentences to create suspension and to help express how she was feeling. It makes it seem like her mind cannot think further than a few words.

This makes little sense and is not supported in any way.

Drifts into vague, irrelevant comments.

Examiner comment

This answer struggles to get beyond simple spotting, although it does start reasonably well and uses the text to support the idea that the course is frightening and 'deadly'. There are some relevant quotations but the analysis of 'how' becomes less assured as the answer goes on. The ending is weak and drifts into vague, formulaic comments. There is no mention of the sense of speed and how that is shown. This is grade D.

GradeStudio

Student 2

Sensible opening and gets the main point.

Good supporting quotation with some comment.

Neat use of text to support this point.

Not a bad attempt but the choice of word could be better.

Sees the sense of speed.

Wyatt tries to get across how difficult and dangerous it is to ride the TT. She says, 'If I let go of the straps I will fall off and break open my head.' This seems very dangerous and makes the reader understand how risky it is. She emphasises the danger by describing the bends as 'evil-looking.' She describes how painful it is to ride the course. She says, 'My head flies forward as if it has been severed by an axe'. Petronella emphasises how scared she is by repeating the word 'graveyard'. This suggests there are so many of them there must be lots of deaths, showing how dangerous and frightening an ordeal it must be. She describes how 'sweat is trickling down her arms'. This emphasises how uncomfortable the ride must be and also shows how nervous she was.

She emphasises how fast they were going by saying 'scenery seems to be zooming towards me.' Furthermore, she tries to put across the danger by telling us about a sign she saw which said, 'Be very careful. 164 casualties in 3 years'.

Not quite the point of this.

Sensible choice of detail from the text.

Sees the repetition of 'graveyard' and its significance.

Uses 'this suggests' to develop the point well.

Another useful detail from the text.

Good supporting evidence, although there is more to find.

Returns to danger but it is well supported.

Examiner comment

This answer clearly gets the sense of speed and danger and uses the text well to show how the writer is communicating those feelings to the reader. Quotation is used quite purposefully to provide evidence and there is some attempt to say 'how' the writer is making her points. The most obvious weakness in this answer is the failure to mention that at the end of the ride the writer felt a real sense of excitement and was thrilled by the experience. There is some potential here, but it is not thorough enough in its coverage and there is no sophisticated grasp of the techniques the writer is using. This is grade C.

Persuasive techniques: how to go up the grades

To move up the grades you need to focus on the question, but above all, you need to stay close to the text and select and use relevant details. Some of these will certainly be content, some will almost certainly be language, and you may be able to identify and try to analyse other techniques.

Try to develop your skill in using short quotations and weaving them into your answer. Student 1 fell into the trap of vague, 'formulaic' comments.

The best of the answers showed a sound technique and clear understanding, and it should be reassuring to see that a methodical approach which moves fluently from evidence to comment (or vice versa) will work. Follow the sequence of the text and take the relevant points as you find them.

Putting it into practice

On your own or with a partner, explain what you now know about:

- identifying the persuasive techniques in a text
- supporting your ideas by reference to the content of the text
- supporting your ideas by selecting and analysing key words and phrases
- identifying other techniques used to persuade
- what makes the difference between a grade D answer and a grade C answer.

In the future

- You must practise this type of question using a range of texts.
- Use details and words/phrases to support your answer.
- Make sure you give specific examples of any techniques you identify.
- Always work methodically through the text.
- Aim to produce a complete answer in 10–15 minutes.

My learning objectives ▼

● to practise analysing persuasive writing
● to develop a secure technique for answering this type of question.

Exam practice and assessment

When answering questions on persuasive techniques, remember to identify and comment on the techniques used, supporting your ideas by referring to the text and analysing key words and phrases.

Activity 1

Read the article and answer the question on persuasive techniques below.

How does David Hunn try to show the 'madness' of the TT races? (10 marks)

IT'S A MAD, MAD WORLD

■ **BY DAVID HUNN**

Welcome to Mad Sunday on the Isle of Man. Yesterday was the serious Formula 1 stuff, but today is for the crazy amateurs. They will be at it soon after dawn and the TT circuit will, as usual, be ridden by
5 any wildcat on two wheels who fancies his chances of surviving an encounter with the bumps and banks, the poles and pillars of these 38 twisting miles. No fairground switchback is more erratic, no wall of death more deadly. And many of the riders will, in their wild
10 enthusiasm, try to hurl themselves around it at 120 mph, even 150 mph on the straights – whatever they can force out of their powerful machines.

The authorities do their best to reduce the numbers indulging in this chaos by staging
15 alternative entertainments, but they will not dissuade the determined. There was even a serious suggestion this year that a speed limit be imposed, but such interference was dismissed.

Nothing on the motorcycling calendar so excites
20 the real enthusiast as these two weeks on the Isle of Man, which calls itself the road-racing capital of the world. The nine races have attracted 540 entries from 19 nations, but that is only the magnet. The iron filings fill the ferry from Lancashire for days on end.
25 Last year the outrageously expensive boats carried 11,500 bikes, 2,700 cars and 30,000 passengers. That doubles the population, and hoteliers, who

struggle to keep their heads above water through the rest of the year, rub their hands, air the beds, whack up the prices and tolerate being overrun by 30 black leather and gleaming metal.

THE TIMES

This is the oldest racing circuit in the world and the first TT race was in 1907 when the fastest lap speed was less than 43 mph. Steve Hislop, this year's favourite,
35 averaged more than 123 mph – close to the record – on a practice lap on Monday. Last year, Mark Farmer rode his Yamaha to the eighth fastest lap in history on the Thursday afternoon. But by Thursday evening he was dead, ending a bright career in a horrific crash at
40 Bedstead Corner.

A local journalist believes that more than 170 have died on the Isle of Man since the races began. There were ten last year, including spectators, the blame for which is shared between organisers, the riders, and
45 those who dangle perilously close to the action.

Crashes are too frequent to count and this year there were six in the first practice on Monday. The local hospital is on emergency alert, served by a helicopter at the course that brings in at least 20 serious injuries each
50 year. Death is discreetly parcelled away and statistics are not kept, they say.

'Dangerous? Yes, it's very dangerous,' says Steve Hislop, who travels at close to 200 mph on some sections of the course. 'At that speed your eyeballs are
55 jumping about in their sockets and you can see a dozen of everything. Anyone who says he isn't glad when it's over is telling lies. But it is still the biggest challenge of the lot, to man and machine. And it's the only event in the UK with decent prize money.' ∎

Peer/Self-assessment

1 Check your answers to Activity 1.
- Did you find a range of techniques?
- Did you work through all of the text in a clear sequence?
- Did you find evidence in the text to support each of your comments?
- Did you find any examples of particular words and phrases used by the writer to influence his readers?

2 Now try to grade your answer to Activity 1 using the mark scheme below. You will need to be careful and precise in your marking. Give a tick for each clear comment and a tick for each piece of relevant evidence. The ticks will guide you to the correct mark, but you also need to make a judgement about the quality and coherence of the answer.

⬆ Moving up the grades

A 8–10 marks
- explores appropriate detail from the text with depth and insight
- best answers are thorough and perceptive, covering a range of points accurately and with an assured grasp of the persuasive technique.

C 5–7 marks
- selects appropriate detail from the text to show understanding of 'how' the writer tries to persuade or influence his readers
- better answers move smoothly from comment to evidence
- there is good coverage of the text
- the main points are clearly made
- better answers have a clear focus on the question.

D 2–4 marks
- makes simple comments based on surface features of text
- identifies some obvious techniques
- some relevant detail from the text
- some focus on the question.

My learning objectives ▼

- to learn how to compare and contrast two texts
- to understand how to approach this type of question.

Comparing and contrasting texts

GradeStudio

MAKE THE GRADE

Examiner tip

This type of question does not involve your opinions; you should stay out of the argument. Focus on what the question asks you to do, and nothing else!

In Paper 1 you are required to answer a question (it is usually the last question) that involves looking at two texts. You will be asked to compare and contrast or make 'cross-references'.

The wording of the question varies from year to year, but there are basically two ways of testing your ability to compare and contrast or make 'cross-references'.

'Compare and contrast' questions

These questions ask you to look for specific similarities and differences in the two texts. Your personal views and opinions are not required. You will waste time and get no marks if you ignore the question and simply give your views about the texts or the issues they discuss.

These questions look like this:

> 1 These two texts give very different impressions. In what ways are they different?
>
> 2 Compare and contrast what these two texts tell you about…
>
> 3 These two texts are about… Compare and contrast them using the following headings…

In this type of question you will often be given a list of bullet points to follow, and you should use them to structure your answer. If you are told to organise your answer into paragraphs using the bullet points as headings, then you should do exactly that. Remember that the examiner is trying to help you and you should take whatever help is offered.

Comparing and contrasting is a skill that requires clarity of thought and organisation. The candidates who handle this type of question well are those who can stand back and see the broad picture. The supporting detail from the text can then be used purposefully. Try to avoid including personal views and opinions which can lead to long but unfocused answers.

Sometimes it is possible to see that both texts are making the same point and it is economical when you can claim that 'both texts' say this. However, don't force the similarities. There will probably be differences too.

The more obvious approach is to state clearly what one text or writer is saying and then to state what the second text or writer has to say on the same topic.

It is useful to create a table to help you to see the similarities and differences between the two texts.

Extract 1	Extract 2

Daily Mail

THE FASTEST LADY ON TWO WHEELS!

Early the next morning, Simon introduces me to Milky. […] He is on the weedy side, with watery eyes and a pale face with a dreamy expression. […]

[…] We go over and look at the bikes. They are monstrous. […]

Fortunately, I see a smaller, safer-looking machine in the corner that resembles more of a motorised bicycle.

'I'll ride that one,' I say.

'But that's a 1907 bike,' protests Simon. 'It only goes up to 25mph.'

'That's why I'll ride it.' Milky is having none of it […] and I am dragged over to a gargantuan Suzuki 1000. Milky takes the bike over to the grandstand.

[…] I notice that the starting line is opposite a graveyard. This rather does for my composure […] but Milky is on the bike, raring to go. […]

I put on my crash helmet and clamber onto the pillion seat […].

Milky is wearing straps around his waist, which I am supposed to hold on to. […]

I am instructed to punch him if I become nervous. He has evidently never taken a course in logic. In order to punch him, I would have to let go of the straps. If I let go of the straps I will fall off and break open my head.

It is, as the youth of today would say, a no-brainer. Unfortunately, that seems to be exactly what Milky is as well.

He revs up and we head towards a village on the north-east shore. Before us is a series of evil-looking bends.

Suddenly, Milky drops his elbow and opens the throttle. I am nearly thrown over the front of the bike.

Ahead of us is Ballaugh Bridge. Ballaugh Bridge is no laughing matter. t has seen eight fatalities in three years. 'Stop going so fast,' I scream at Milky. He accelerates. Then […] he decides to brake. My head flies forward as if it has been severed by an axe.

'I just thought I'd stop [...] areas of interest on the c[...] explains. 'We are just abou[...] Ballagarey Corner. It is on[...] dangerous on the villag[...] continues cheerfully, 'On[...] there.'

'Lost him? You me[...] wrong turning?'

'No, he crashed and [...] coffin.'

We round the corne[...] Sweat is trickling dow[...]

Another graveyar[...] this island consist o[...] Finally, we leave [...] Mountain Course. [...]

Milky tells me w[...] speed that to any b[...] blur. I say I do no[...] can see the obituar[...] 'A blur died yester[...] the Isle of Man T[...]

But there is no [...] who is not only [...] convinced I am [...]

passenger […].

The mountain course dips and swerves […] and there are boulders and abysses everywhere.

I see a few sheep. I suppose if I have to land on anything, I would rather it was a [...] As Milky opens the throttle again, [...]raging

IT'S A MAD, MAD WORLD

■ **BY DAVID HUNN**

Welcome to Mad Sunday on the Isle of Man. Yesterday was the serious Formula 1 stuff, but today is for the crazy amateurs. They will be at it soon after dawn and the TT circuit will, as usual, be ridden by any wildcat on two wheels who fancies his chances of surviving an encounter with the bumps and banks, the poles and pillars of these 38 twisting miles. No fairground switchback is more erratic, no wall of death more deadly. And many of the riders will, in their wild enthusiasm, try to hurl themselves around it at 120 mph, even 150 mph on the straights – whatever they can force out of their powerful machines.

The authorities do their best to reduce the numbers indulging in this chaos by staging alternative entertainments, but they will not dissuade the determined. There was even a serious suggestion this year that a speed limit be imposed, but such interference was dismissed.

Nothing on the motorcycling calendar so excites the real enthusiast as these two weeks on the Isle of Man, which calls itself the road-racing capital of the world. The nine races have attracted 540 entries from 19 nations, but that is only the magnet. The iron filings fill the ferry from Lancashire for days on end. Last year the outrageously expensive boats carried 11,500 bikes, 2,700 cars and 30,000 passengers. That doubles the population, and hoteliers, who struggle to keep their heads above water through the rest of the year, rub their hands, air the beds, whack up the prices and tolerate being overrun by black leather and gleaming metal.

Activity 1

1 Read the two student responses below and then, on your own or with a partner, answer the following questions.
- What are the two writers' attitudes to the smoking ban?
- What reasons do they give for their attitudes?

Extract 1

Last year a ban on smoking in public places was enforced in England and Wales. I don't think I have ever seen a bigger mistake in my life. The logic behind the whole idea is undeniably sound, but, when put into practice, a number of
5 flaws are shown.

Banning smoking at football matches, concerts, on trains or buses I can understand, but banning it from pubs, I don't understand. To people who complain about people smoking in pubs whilst they are drinking, I have a simple solution – just
10 move to the other side of the bar or go outside. When people go into the pub it is to relax and unwind and if smoking helps you do that then fine.

Because of this ban the smokers have been forced out on to the streets and every time I wander past my local pub I am
15 forced to squeeze through the crowd of smokers just to get to the other end of the pavement.

I don't smoke. I think it is a filthy, disgusting habit, but I have got absolutely nothing against other people smoking. If
20 it annoyed me I would just move away. That is why I think banning smoking at football matches was a good thing because most of the time you can't move away, but at a pub you can just go to the other end of the bar or out into the garden. You shouldn't force people out onto the street like
25 outcasts. It's just wrong.

I ask you, have they really done anything so wrong that they have to be removed from certain areas of society? I will tell you the answer it is no. Smoking is not a crime, yet we are treating smokers like they have done something deeply wrong.

Extract 2

Everybody understands the risks of smoking – indeed, they have been publicised well enough, and even introduced into the National Curriculum. It is obvious that smoking carries an overwhelming danger to human health, but I understand its
5 addictiveness and the right of individual choice. However, individual freedom – no matter how 'well publicised' it is – should never infringe on the rights of others, something which smoking in public places certainly does.

Second-hand smoking is the cause of over 10,500 deaths
10 annually. It may just be a number, but we must think of these 10,500 people – with hopes, dreams and fears – destroyed by something that was, ultimately, not under their control. It may sound melodramatic, over-the-top, clichéd but think about it. One in three of us will be affected – individually or through
15 family or friends – by smoking-related disease. How many of those affected have been irrevocably damaged by second-hand smoke? These 10,500 had families, lovers, friends – who's to say that you won't be next?

We must stop thinking about smoking diseases as something
20 which could never happen to us. Distancing ourselves from the problem will only increase its severity. How often did you used to go out, before the smoking ban? How often would you frequent bars, cinemas, restaurants where smokers could casually puff away at a cigarette, probably oblivious to the
25 damage they were doing? People have to realise the tangible danger of second-hand smoke, before it's too late.

2 Now try this on your own:
Compare and contrast the views of these two writers on the subject of the ban on smoking in public places.

GradeStudio

Here are two student responses to the exam question below (about the articles on pages 76 and 80–81). Read the answers together with the examiner comments, then check what you have learnt and try putting it into practice.

'It's A Mad, Mad World' and 'The Fastest Lady on Two Wheels' are both about the TT (Tourist Trophy) races on the Isle of Man.

Compare and contrast what the writers think about them.

Organise your answer into <u>two</u> paragraphs using the following headings:
- **What they think about the TT circuit**
- **What they think about the riders**

A | grade answer

Student 1

What they think about the TT circuit

Petronella Wyatt describes the circuit as 'the most dangerous in the world'. She describes it as 'the jaws of hell'. She says the course has 'evil-looking bends' and 'consists only of graveyards'. She does not feel comfortable and seems convinced she will fall off and crash and imagines her obituary. She says the course is on dangerous ground and thinks she is about to pass out. At the end, however, she feels 'a massive surge of adrenaline' and doesn't want it to stop. She feels immense ecstasy and obviously enjoyed the experience, forgetting the fear she had felt during it.

David Hunn believes that the circuit is 'erratic' and that 'no wall of death is more deadly'. He describes it as 'chaos' but that nothing so 'excites the real enthusiast'. He seems to think the circuit is dangerous and spectators are 'perilously close' to the race. He says that 'crashes are too frequent to count' and obviously believes there are too many deaths.

What they think about the riders

Wyatt is not too complimentary of her driver, describing him as 'on the weedy side'. She judges him on appearance and says he has 'watery eyes and a pale face'. She says that he is 'raring to go'. She is sarcastic about Milky, saying he has 'evidently never taken a course in logic'. Later on, she describes him as talking 'cheerfully' of a friend's death. She says he is high on adrenaline. Overall she is not very positive about him.

David Hunn believes the riders are 'crazy amateurs'. He also describes them as 'determined' and 'real enthusiasts'. He describes the death of one of the 'wildcats', describing it as a 'horrific crash' which ended a 'bright career'. He seems to believe the riders are responsible for the deaths of some spectators. He seems to imply that the only reason a professional rider does it is for 'the decent prize money'.

Examiner comment

This answer contains more than two paragraphs, but it is organised into two sections under clear headings. This helps to keep the answer focused on the question and avoids a lot of irrelevant material finding its way into the answer. Notice that the student looks at each writer in turn and sees that Wyatt and Hunn both think that the course is dangerous and that Wyatt also felt the thrill of the course. There is some good supporting detail here and the only point missed is that both writers comment on the frightening speed of the course. The section on the riders is focused and detailed and uses the text neatly to show exactly what the two writers feel about the riders. This is grade A.

A* grade answer

Student 2

What they think about the TT circuit

Both writers agree that the course is dangerous. Wyatt refers to 'the jaws of hell' and Hunn compares it to 'a wall of death'. Both writers also think it is very, very fast with speeds of up to 200mph. However, Wyatt does eventually find it thrilling and experiences a 'surge of adrenaline' as she rides it.

What they think about the riders

Both writers think that the riders are mad. Wyatt calls Milky a 'no-brainer' and Hunn refers to 'crazy amateurs'. Wyatt thinks Milky is fearless and oblivious to danger, but Hunn quotes Steve Hislop who says that he is glad when it is over, implying he is scared. Wyatt thinks Milky is a thrill-seeker, high on adrenaline, but Hunn suggests that the riders are motivated by the 'decent prize money'.

Examiner summary

This answer also follows the instructions in the question exactly. It is concise and clear and never loses sight of what the question is asking. It pulls together that both writers think the course is dangerous and then provides just enough evidence from the texts to clinch the point. It moves clearly into the point that both writers think the course is very fast, again with just a snippet of evidence to support the point. However, what makes this answer so good is that it sees that it is only really Wyatt who finds it thrilling.

The section about the riders is also concise and focused, making comments about 'both' writers when they are valid and accurate, but also making contrasts with concise reference to the texts. This answer has the clarity of thought and organisation that demands full marks. Grade A*.

MOVING UP THE GRADES

Comparing and contrasting texts: how to go up the grades

As you have seen with these examples of students' work, to move up the grades you must read the question carefully and do exactly what it tells you to do. You will usually be told how to organise and present your answer and you must do it that way. Make it easy for the examiner to see that you are answering the question. Students 1 and 2 both took the help in the question.

You can point out that both writers say, or think, something, but don't force it and be prepared to show the contrasts in opinion. Use the texts to give some support to your answer but don't get too bogged down in aimless or irrelevant material. Keep a clear focus on what the question is asking you to do.

Putting it into practice

On your own or with a partner, explain what you now know about:
- making comparisons and contrasts across two texts
- supporting your ideas by reference to the texts
- organising and presenting your answer
- what makes the difference between a grade A answer and a grade A* answer.

In the future

- You must practise this type of question using a range of texts.
- Always follow the instructions in the question.
- Make sure you focus only on what you are asked to do.
- Look for similarities but also differences.
- Select and use examples from the texts but don't overdo it.
- Aim to produce a complete answer in 10–15 minutes.

My learning objectives ▼

- to use information from two texts
- to learn how to approach this type of question.

Using information from two texts

In Paper 1 you are required to answer a question that involves looking at two texts (it is usually the last question). You will be asked to compare and contrast, as we have already seen, or make 'cross-references'.

The second way of testing your ability to make cross-references between texts is to ask you to find relevant information using both texts. This type of question is used less frequently than the 'compare and contrast' approach, but you need to know how to tackle it.

'Using information from two texts' questions

To answer this type of question, you must focus on what you have been asked to find. It usually makes sense to identify where you found the information. You will waste time and get no marks if you ignore the question and simply give your views about the texts or the issues they discuss.

These questions look like this:

▶ Using information from both texts, explain…

▶ Using information from both texts, identify what…

▶ Using information from both texts, say what…

It is sensible to start with one text and then to tackle the second text. Don't try to dart from one text to the other. You might find it helpful to create a table which will help focus your thinking, for example.

Extract 1	Extract 2

Activity 1

Look at the two extracts on pages 90 and 91. We will use them to get started with this type of question.

On your own or with a partner, note down the relevant information in each extract to answer the question below.

Using information from both texts, make a list of tips for parents on how to cope with teenagers.

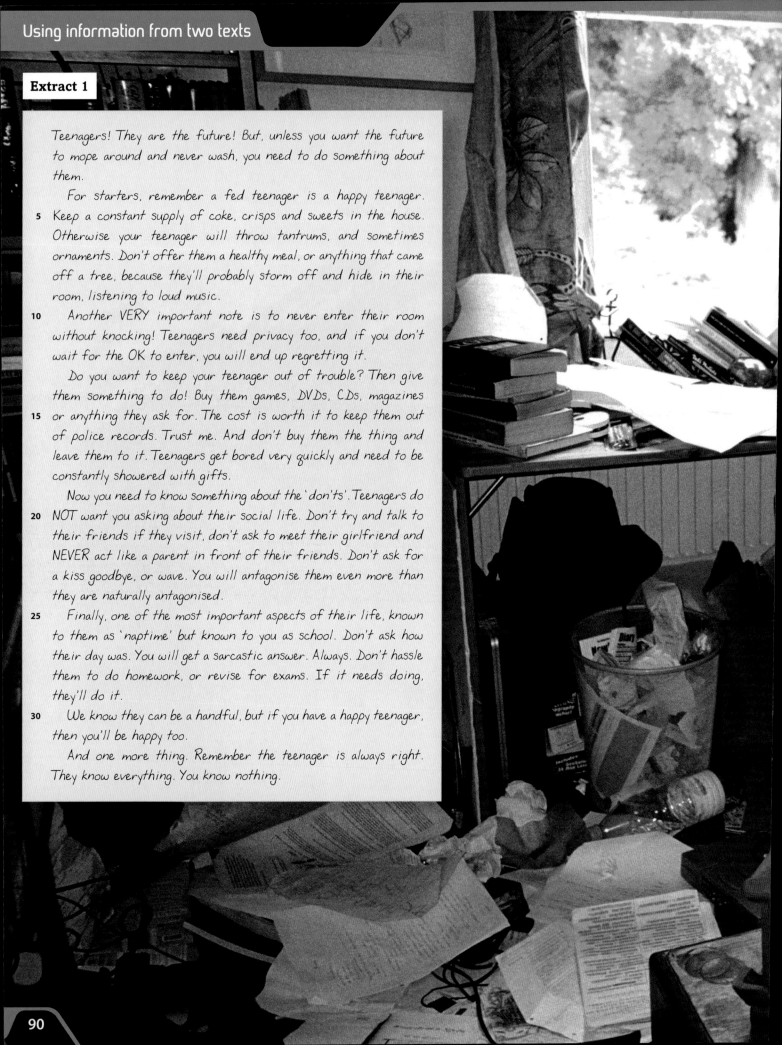

Extract 1

Teenagers! They are the future! But, unless you want the future to mope around and never wash, you need to do something about them.

For starters, remember a fed teenager is a happy teenager.
5 Keep a constant supply of coke, crisps and sweets in the house. Otherwise your teenager will throw tantrums, and sometimes ornaments. Don't offer them a healthy meal, or anything that came off a tree, because they'll probably storm off and hide in their room, listening to loud music.

10 Another VERY important note is to never enter their room without knocking! Teenagers need privacy too, and if you don't wait for the OK to enter, you will end up regretting it.

Do you want to keep your teenager out of trouble? Then give them something to do! Buy them games, DVDs, CDs, magazines
15 or anything they ask for. The cost is worth it to keep them out of police records. Trust me. And don't buy them the thing and leave them to it. Teenagers get bored very quickly and need to be constantly showered with gifts.

Now you need to know something about the 'don'ts'. Teenagers do
20 NOT want you asking about their social life. Don't try and talk to their friends if they visit, don't ask to meet their girlfriend and NEVER act like a parent in front of their friends. Don't ask for a kiss goodbye, or wave. You will antagonise them even more than they are naturally antagonised.

25 Finally, one of the most important aspects of their life, known to them as 'naptime' but known to you as school. Don't ask how their day was. You will get a sarcastic answer. Always. Don't hassle them to do homework, or revise for exams. If it needs doing, they'll do it.

30 We know they can be a handful, but if you have a happy teenager, then you'll be happy too.

And one more thing. Remember the teenager is always right. They know everything. You know nothing.

Extract 2

Basically, from the 13th birthday to the 21st birthday, hide! There is no stopping the teenage genie from infecting your child, so get the most out of the preteen years as you have no hope of getting civil conversation for the next eight years.

5 You may be lucky and have a child who stops being a teenager at eighteen, but you will still get the boozing and partying of a teenager, just with better conversation.

The biggest shock to you would be the sudden and deadly mood swings. EXIT THE ROOM. Don't make eye contact, just
10 back away slowly and close the door behind you. There is no point confronting them when they are like this because their brains are currently going into meltdown so all rational thought is lost.

Arguments with teenagers are long, loud and not forgotten.
15 Teenagers are unable to see your point of view and suggesting to them that what they want to do might cause worry to you, or is not pleasant, sends them into confusion and stress as their brains cannot cope with two things at once. Therefore it is easier for them to try and make YOU see THEIR point
20 of view.

They will make the four walls their 'nest' and I suggest not going in there. I can almost guarantee that there will be clothes on the floor and rubbish overflowing the bin. And, if you have a boy, it would be very dark 'so I can see the computer
25 screen'. Only enter when they are out because they would respond to your shock by simply saying 'I've got GCSEs. You don't understand!' Please, save yourself the stress and DO NOT ENTER.

I wish you the best of luck with your teenager. I suggest
30 you read 'The Book of grunts and what they mean'. The road to heaven is narrow and twisty and they will return to civilisation eventually so, hang on in there!

On pages 94–95 are three student responses to the exam question below. Read the answers together with the examiner comments, then check what you have learnt and try putting it into practice.

Using information from both texts, explain what you learn about the relationship between Fogle and Cracknell during the race. (10 marks)

These two texts are about Ben Fogle, a television presenter, and James Cracknell, an Olympic gold medallist in rowing. In 2005 they had competed in a race to row across the Atlantic Ocean.

Extract 1

Interview with James Cracknell

Since last Saturday, we have hardly made any progress – just 100 miles in almost a week. We've experienced the worst weather they've ever had in the race and it looks as if it will
5 continue until next Tuesday.

The hurricane itself didn't hit us, but we got caught by strong winds blowing in exactly the wrong direction so we had to put down the sea anchor. For two and a half days, we were stuck
10 in our cabin, which is like being shut in a car boot. When the wind eased off, we were able to set off at midnight and row for seven hours, which took us over the 2000 miles-to-go mark. We celebrated with a chocolate bar. But we
15 keep having to stop because of the weather.

We've lost so many days that we are starting having to ration our food. We wanted to do the race in 40 days and took enough food for 50, but that looks optimistic now, so we've cut our
20 daily ration of 8000–9000 calories by 500–600. By the time we get to the last few days, we will be having a horrible time because we've left all the food we don't like until then.

We've been thirsty as well as hungry. Earlier
25 in the week, the desalinator broke and we nearly had to break into the fresh water we carry as ballast. […] We could only drink five to six litres a day, instead of ten.

We haven't seen another boat since the day we set off so we don't know our position in the 30 race, but I expect others have pulled ahead […]. The weather has brought out the differences in our competitive attitudes, so there has been a bit of tension. I mind about being overtaken and I'm keener to row in the rain than Ben is; he just 35 wants to get to the end.

I'm not looking forward to the next four days because we're going to be stuck in the cabin again. We're bored with talking to each other, we've only got one pack of cards and we've 40 played all the games we know.

We need to sleep as much as we can, but it gets really hot in the cabin because the wind is so strong that we have to keep the windows and hatch shut. Out of a twelve-hour night, we 45 probably sleep for only two hours, and spend the rest of the night trying to get comfortable. We sleep head to toe on a shelf that is only the width of a shoulder and, just as I am dozing off, I find Ben's foot in my mouth. 50

Heart-throbs of the High Seas

The men worked in two-hour shifts. While one rowed, the other would sleep for 90 minutes in the tiny, airless cabin that felt, Fogle says, 'like a coffin'. Then they would get up, wash, eat and prepare to take the oars for the next two hours. They repeated this routine 24 hours a day, seven days a week, for the best part
5 of two months.

It might, then, have been useful had Fogle learned to row beforehand. 'Part of me thought, "Well, rowing can't be that hard"…' Fogle starts. Cracknell interrupts sarcastically to point out that 'it's not that hard, but it does take a lot of practice.'

'Exactly, practice,' Fogle replies. 'And I thought if there's anywhere I'm going
10 to learn, it's at sea spending months in a rowing boat.'

Cracknell looks at him bemusedly. It is their relationship – and the differences between the two men – that lies at the heart of their journey […]. Fogle describes himself as a 'take-parter'; Cracknell is obsessed with winning. Fogle wants to quit following their capsize; Cracknell won't hear of it. They have monumental
15 arguments over the water supply, and Fogle gets so angry with Cracknell that at one point, he attempts to break the seat.

'We had a lot of blazing rows,' says Fogle. 'But after the capsize, when we didn't have the satellite phone and couldn't speak to relatives, we had to speak to each other. We'd always known we relied on each other to get through this,
20 but it was only after that I fully realised it was a friendship.'

Cracknell recalls one moment when they had a huge barney which culminated in Fogle telling him that he'd hated being on the boat with him.

'It really did hurt,' he says. 'It made me realise how much I enjoyed his company. I learned that there's a side to him that's very different from me. It was at that
25 moment that I realised our friendship would go beyond the race.'

THE SCOTSMAN

GradeStudio

Student 1

<u>Their relationship during the race</u>

In the telephone interview, Cracknell said there was 'tension' between them because they are very different when it comes to competing. He said they were 'bored' with talking to each other so they had nothing to say to each other. The newspaper article describes the 'monumental arguments' and 'blazing rows' that they had. However, they had to speak to each other when they lost the phone and they relied on each other to get through so they became close.

Examiner comment

This answer is quite brief but it has a decent focus on the question. Some valid points are made and there is a clear attempt to identify the texts and say where the information was found. The mention of 'tension' is sensible and the student tries to explain exactly what was causing the difficulty in the relationship. The use of the two quotations – 'blazing rows' and 'monumental arguments' – is quite neat and the point about them having to talk to each other when they lost the phone is handled clearly. The answer does not do much to develop the point about the two men becoming close, but it is made clearly enough. There is more to say, but this answer shows understanding and some sensible detail. This is a secure grade C.

Student 2

Both the interview and the newspaper article emphasise the fact that the two men did not get on well during the race. There was 'tension' between them and they had 'blazing rows' and 'monumental arguments'. They grew 'bored' with each other. However, they needed each other to get through the race and they realised that they were just different. Cracknell admitted that he liked Fogle's company and that they would stay friends when the race was over.

Examiner comment

This answer chooses not to identify the texts, but it is coherent and shows clear understanding of what the two texts have to say about the relationship between the two men. It immediately makes the point that they did not get on well, and uses evidence from both texts to support the point. It picks up the point made by Cracknell that they got bored with each other. The use of 'however' signals the change in the relationship and the fact that the men began to accept their differences and develop a lasting friendship is made clearly. This answer is clear and sensible and sees 'the big picture' quite well. This would be awarded a grade B.

Student 3

<u>Their relationship during the race</u>

In the telephone interview Cracknell admits they had different 'competitive attitudes' and this caused 'tension' after a while. Fogle wanted to quit after the capsize but Cracknell would not hear of it. They became 'bored' with talking to each other. The article suggests that the relationship was worse than just 'tense' but was very strained as they had 'monumental arguments' and 'blazing rows'. They got really angry with each other – they had a 'huge barney' – and at one point Fogle got so furious that he tried to break the seat. He hurt Cracknell when he told him he 'hated' being on the boat with him. However, they relied on each other to get through the race, particularly when they lost the phone and had to talk to each other, and Cracknell realised that 'there's a side to him that's very different'. This strengthened their relationship. Cracknell also realised that he enjoyed Fogle's company and that their friendship would last beyond the race.

Examiner comment

This answer is sharp, but it has clarity and it is well structured, using paragraphs to guide the reader and give the answer some shape. It begins with the Cracknell interview and selects textual evidence neatly to convey the 'tension' and problems in the relationship. It then moves to the article and makes an explicit cross-reference, suggesting that the problems went beyond 'tension' and 'boredom'. The relevant details are well selected and the answer picks out and develops all of the available evidence. The final paragraph uses 'however' to show the change in the relationship, and this is also explained clearly with good supporting detail. This would be awarded an A*.

Using information from two texts: how to go up the grades

To move up the grades you must refer to both texts and select the relevant points clearly. You need to see the 'big picture' and choose your evidence carefully, focusing consistently on what you have been asked to do.

Notice that the first answer is too brief and misses a vital development in the relationship between the two men. The second answer goes up the grades because of its clarity and coherence, but the final answer combines relevant detail from the text with thorough explanation.

Putting it into practice

On your own or with a partner, explain what you now know about:

- finding information across two texts
- supporting your ideas by reference to the texts
- organising and presenting your answer
- what makes the difference between a grade C answer and a grade A* answer.

In the future

- You must practise this type of question using a range of texts.
- Always follow the instructions in the question.
- Make sure you focus only on what you are asked to do.
- Look for similarities but also differences.
- Select and use examples from the texts, but don't overdo it.
- Aim to produce a complete answer in 10–15 minutes.

2 Writing information and ideas

What will the Writing paper look like?

In this paper you will have 1 hour to attempt two pieces of transactional writing – writing that pays special attention to audience, purpose and format. Both answers will be marked out of 20. You will be asked to write in two different forms, for example: a letter, a report, an article, a leaflet, a speech/talk or a review.

This paper will test your writing skills, including the presentation of your work, sentence structure, punctuation, spelling and layout. About two-thirds of the marks are awarded for what you say and the organisation of your work, and the other third for the accuracy of your writing.

What will the questions be like?

The questions will test your ability to do some of the following: to argue a case, to explain something, to persuade someone to do something, to give advice, to comment on an issue or to write a review. Obviously different questions will require you to do different things, and the two questions in this paper may test different skills. Unlike the writing you will undertake for controlled assessment (which may include descriptive, narrative and first- and third-person writing), this is functional writing – things you could well find yourself doing in real life. If you have already attempted the Functional English Writing paper, you will find the activities here very similar.

What should I do?

▶ Read the instructions carefully – they are there to help you.

▶ Divide your time equally, i.e. about 30 minutes per question, and make sure your answers are about the length suggested. You will lose marks if you offer brief responses.

▶ Read the questions carefully and make sure that you answer the question set.

▶ Think carefully before you write – plan what you will say in your introduction, in each paragraph and in the conclusion.

▶ Think carefully about your audience before you start to write.

▶ When you have finished writing, read through your work and check for errors – don't be afraid to make changes if they will improve your work.

How will I be assessed?

The examiner will assess your answers against the assessment criteria outlined on page 5.

Writing paper sample question types

Below are some examples of the types of question you could be asked in the Writing paper. These will help you understand what you are preparing for as you work through this section of the book.

1 Informal letters

You have moved with your family to a different part of the country. Write a letter to a close friend, inviting him/her to stay with you. Explain how you would be able to fill your time during the two- to three-day stay.

2 Formal letters

You have read a letter in your local newspaper which suggests that teenagers are rude, lazy and poorly educated. Write to the newspaper giving your views.

A company is offering sponsorship to allow selected students to spend time travelling abroad. You are interested. Write a letter to the company to persuade it that you would be the right person to make the most of this opportunity.

3 Reports

Because of the present economic problems your school/college has received less money than last year and has to make cuts. Write a report to the headteacher/principal, indicating where you would make savings but also indicating things that should be protected.

4 Articles for newspapers and magazines

Write an entertaining article for a teenage magazine about life since you have become a teenager. Remember that the purpose of the article is to entertain.

5 Leaflets

The government is keen for students to remain in full-time education after completing their GCSEs. Write a leaflet persuading them to stay at school or to join a local college.

6 Speeches/talks

As part of your Speaking and Listening activities you have been asked to talk to your class about your two/three choices for Room 101. Write what you would say.

7 Reviews

Write a review of a film or television programme you have recently watched for a newspaper or magazine. You may decide where it will appear.

Write a review of a book or CD you have particularly enjoyed. Your review will appear in a teenage magazine.

What will I learn about transactional writing?

You will learn about:

▶ the different questions set on transactional writing – letters, reports, newspaper and magazine articles, leaflets, speeches, and reviews

▶ the layout of the different pieces of writing

▶ the need to adopt the right tone in your writing

▶ the content of the different questions

▶ some different ways of approaching the questions

▶ how to think about your audience and purpose.

In transactional writing the emphasis is on audience and purpose, and, in some cases, format. So what do we mean by these three things?

Audience

This means the person or people you are writing for. It could be a friend, a potential employer, your class, a newspaper/magazine reader, a relation, etc. What you write and the way you write it will be determined by who the reader is. For a friend, your tone will be friendly, chatty and informal (bearing in mind that you are writing in an exam). For an employer, on the other hand, you will adopt a more formal tone.

Purpose

This means the reason for the piece of writing – for example, to argue a point of view, to persuade, comment, explain or review. You may write a letter to a newspaper on a subject of concern to your local area, or write an article for a teenage magazine, or write what you would say to your class in a Speaking and Listening activity. You may be required to write a leaflet or factsheet telling people about an issue that interests you. Remember that these are all based on real-life situations.

Format

Format means how you set something out. When writing a letter, make sure that you include an address/addresses, the date, a salutation such as 'Dear' and an ending or a closure (for example 'Yours faithfully' or 'Yours sincerely' if the letter is formal, or 'Love' for someone you are close to).

A report contains headings and sub-headings so that different topics are dealt with separately and so that the report is easier to follow and therefore more effective. Similarly, newspaper/magazine articles, leaflets, factsheets and reviews will have headings (possibly catchy ones) and perhaps sub-sections. Photographs and diagrams may be indicated, but don't waste time drawing them. Remember you are being judged on your writing skills.

Writing an informal letter

My learning objectives ▼

- to learn about the layout and organisation of an informal letter
- to learn how style, tone and content work together to achieve effect.

GradeStudio

Examiner tips

- Read the question carefully.
- Plan your answer before you start writing.
- Think in terms of paragraphs – introduction, development and conclusion.
- Remember your audience.
- Your tone will be informal but not casual.
- You have 60 minutes to answer two writing questions, so divide your time equally as both questions carry the same number of marks.
- One third of the marks are awarded for sentence structure, punctuation and spelling, so be careful to get these right!

An informal letter is one sent to someone you know or someone you are familiar with. The letter will be about things you might discuss with a friend or an acquaintance. The degree of informality used will depend on how well you know the recipient. Some of the best informal letters will sound like a friend talking to a friend.

Activity 1

1 Note down a list of occasions when you might need to write an informal letter.

2 What are the features of an informal letter, (for example informal language, a friendly approach)? Use the notes below to help you.

Audience	In this type of letter you will probably be writing to a friend or a member of your family. The language and tone will be informal with a friendly approach, and the letter may have a chatty tone.
Purpose	This will be to keep in touch with someone you know or, perhaps, are related to. You will give information and enquire about things that are of mutual interest, family matters, gossip etc. Though e-mails and text messages are also used for this purpose, a letter is an opportunity to write at greater length and perhaps in a more appropriate tone.
Format	You need to include your address and the date. The salutation will be informal with use of the first or familiar name, e.g. 'Dear Mum' or 'Dear Amit'. The closure will be informal, such as 'Love from'.
Content	The question will tell you what the content should be but whatever the topic, you must plan your letter. Think about your opening paragraph and then about the central points and how you intend to organise what you want to say. Putting across your points logically is important and strengthens your letter. Put yourself in the position of the recipient.

Below is an example of the layout of an informal letter. The annotations
show some of the common features you need to use.

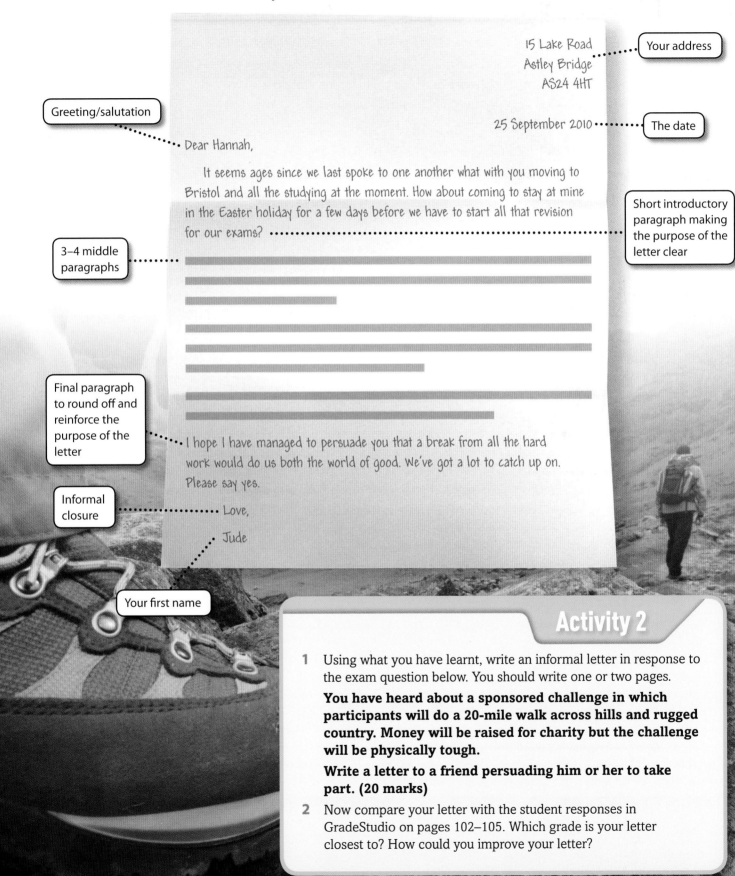

Your address

15 Lake Road
Astley Bridge
AS24 4HT

The date

25 September 2010

Greeting/salutation

Dear Hannah,

It seems ages since we last spoke to one another what with you moving to
Bristol and all the studying at the moment. How about coming to stay at mine
in the Easter holiday for a few days before we have to start all that revision
for our exams?

Short introductory paragraph making the purpose of the letter clear

3–4 middle paragraphs

Final paragraph to round off and reinforce the purpose of the letter

I hope I have managed to persuade you that a break from all the hard
work would do us both the world of good. We've got a lot to catch up on.
Please say yes.

Informal closure

Love,

Jude

Your first name

Activity 2

1   Using what you have learnt, write an informal letter in response to
    the exam question below. You should write one or two pages.

    **You have heard about a sponsored challenge in which
    participants will do a 20-mile walk across hills and rugged
    country. Money will be raised for charity but the challenge
    will be physically tough.**

    **Write a letter to a friend persuading him or her to take
    part. (20 marks)**

2   Now compare your letter with the student responses in
    GradeStudio on pages 102–105. Which grade is your letter
    closest to? How could you improve your letter?

GradeStudio

Here are two informal letters written by students in response to the exam question below. Read the letters together with the examiner comments, then check what you have learnt and try putting it into practice.

You have heard about a sponsored challenge in which participants will do a 20-mile walk across hills and rugged country. Money will be raised for charity but the challenge will be physically tough.

Write a letter to a friend persuading him or her to take part. (20 marks)

You should write one to two pages in your answer book.

D grade answer

Student 1

Dear Dominic,

I am going to be taking part in a walk for charity over hills and rugged country. I was going to ask if you would like to join me doing this, although it will be phisically tough. If you were to take part in this you would get extremley fit and you would raise a lot of money for charity. You could design your own fitness routine that fits into your life or we could do it together? The walk will be twenty miles but if you train properly then I can't see a problem. We can go at our own pace together. I think this would be great for our health and also fun. The charity that we would be raising the money for is Cancer Research UK. I know that we both have had deaths in our families caused by cancer so I think we both owe it to our families to try and put a stop to death by cancer. It would be nice to respect our family members and we could do our walks, dedicated to them. Lots of people from around the country are coming to join this walk. We can also take short breaks to make things easier. I think this would be a great opportunity to get some fresh air and it will be fun. I do hope you join me.

Thank you,

Olivia

Examiner comment

Though this is clearly a letter, very little effort has been made to provide an appropriate layout. However, the purpose is clearly understood and there is an attempt to persuade. The tone of the letter could be more convincing, i.e. the writer does not sound that familiar with Dominic. There is an attempt to conclude the letter though organisation could be a lot better – note the lack of paragraphs and there is some repetition. The letter is also a little brief. Planning before writing could have made a real difference. There are a few errors, though that may be partly because of a lack of ambition. The work was awarded a D grade (6/13 for content and organisation; 3/7 for sentence structure, punctuation and spelling).

Student 2

34 The Close
Harvest Way
Birmingham
B38 4TU

7th January 2010

Hi Sam

Happy New Year! I hope you had a good Christmas and that Santa bought you all of the presents you wanted. Did you and James go to the party you were planning to go to on New Year's Eve?

I remember that last time I saw you said you wanted to get fit this year so I wondered if you would like to take part in a sponsored challenge with me and Lily. It will be really hard but I think it will be fun to train together. The challenge involves lots of walking and outdoors countryside which I know you really enjoy.

The other thing is if we do this we will be raising money for charity so we can help other people as well as getting fit ourselves.

I really hope we can take part in this challenge together, we haven't see each for so long it will be nice to train together and I know that Lily is really excited too.

Hope to hear back from you soon
Say hi to James for me

Love from
Sarah

Examiner comment

The letter is well set out, though there should be a comma after 'Hi Sam'.

The letter starts well in an appropriately friendly tone – the writer and recipient obviously know each other well. The writer then moves into the main point of the letter and explains what its purpose is, covering the challenge of the event as well as the enjoyment. A few sensible/persuasive arguments are made. There is a nice touch at the end continuing the chatty tone of the letter.

This is a competent piece of work; there is good control and a good level of accuracy throughout. The omission of 'you' at the beginning of the second paragraph is one of the very few errors. It's a pity that the student does not provide a more substantial letter but this would be awarded a low B grade in the examination: 7/8 + 5.

GradeStudio

Here is another informal letter written by a student in response to the exam question below. Read the letter together with the examiner comment, then check what you have learnt and try putting it into practice.

You have heard about a sponsored challenge in which participants will do a 20-mile walk across hills and rugged country. Money will be raised for charity but the challenge will be physically tough.

Write a letter to a friend persuading him or her to take part. (20 marks)

You should write one to two pages in your answer book.

A* grade answer

Student 3

> The Clock Tower
> Llangwm
> Pembs
> SA65 4HY
>
> 27 January 2010
>
> Dear Kavita,
>
> How are things at your grandma's house? If it was any further away from here you'd be in Australia! You really need to get your gran into the 21st century and buy her a computer – it took me half an hour just to find an envelope for this. Don't get me started on the stamp. Anyway, I know you are dying to find out what possessed me to write this but I think you'd better sit down first. This could be a bit of a shock. I'm going to do a twenty mile walk for charity and (this is the best part) I want you to do it with me! Are you still breathing? Before you start asking about medication or alien abduction, I am completely sane. I know it sounds tough but I'm sure it will be fine.
>
> So, it's a twenty mile walk across hills and other unimagineable 'little crests' (they look more like Mount Everest though). Yes, twenty miles is further than from here to the bank. A lot further. But, before you send me to a mental hospital, just think about it. How amazing will you look if you can do it? And, I'm sure this will be your favourite part, there are lot of locals already signed up that you can walk behind.
>
> I know it sounds really tough but they're not even going to make us run. It's just a leisurly stroll up a hill and down the other side. Sounds easy, right? Not only will you look like Superwoman but you will truly earn your cape because it raises money for charity. You can even ask Roger to sponsor you. I bet he'll think you're dead brave for doing it.

In fact, why don't you try to get him to try it to? You know what they say, the more the merrier or something like that. He'll have a hard time saying no. Just tell him he'll look weak and he's going to get beaten by a girl. That should do the trick.

I know you hate doing anything that involves moving more than about a metre but please try. Think of how impressed all the lads at school would be. But most of all think about me. You wouldn't leave me to do this all alone, would you?

I know this idea seems hideous and repulsive to you but consider it. It'll grow on you. Help me and help the poor children we are raising money for. Make Superwoman proud. After all (if I dare say it) what's the worst that could happen? Famous last words!

Lots of love and cuddles (you'll need them in Antarctica or wherever you are!)

Love,

Selena xxx

Examiner comment

The layout is generally appropriate. The letter starts well, even clearly explaining why she has resorted to writing a letter. The central paragraphs develop the letter really well and there is a brief but effective conclusion. The witty persuasive tone works well and the clever idea of Superwoman threads its way effectively through the piece. The writing is largely accurate, though there are a few spelling errors. This work is a grade A* (12/13 for content and organisation; 6/7 for sentence structure, punctuation and spelling.)

Informal letters: how to go up the grades

- Show the examiner that you know how to set out an informal letter.
- Plan and organise your work into paragraphs. Don't forget introduction, development and conclusion.
- Remember the purpose of the letter, the stated audience and therefore the tone.
- The letter should be of reasonable length and you will need to develop your thoughts in a clear and interesting way.
- Accuracy is important so take care with sentence structure, punctuation and spelling.

Putting it into practice

Discuss with a classmate what you have learnt in this section. Think about:
- the way in which an informal letter is set out and organised
- how it is different from a formal letter
- the different approaches you could take in a letter on a subject such as inviting a friend to your year's end of term party, or life over here in a letter to your aunt or uncle living abroad.

In the future

- Practise the skills you need to improve.
- Use the checklists provided to help you write a successful informal letter.

My learning objectives ▼

- to practise using key features of an informal letter
- to develop a secure approach to writing an informal letter
- to write with technical accuracy.

Exam practice and assessment

Activity 3

The letter on the right was written in response to the following exam question.

Your grandparents have written to you to ask for suggestions for Christmas presents for your younger sister and brother. Write your letter.

It was awarded a **D** grade in the exam (5/13 for content and organisation and 3/7 for sentence structure, punctuation and spelling), but it would not be difficult to improve on this grade. Use the questions below to suggest ways to improve the letter.

- Can you spot omissions or places where the layout could be improved?
- Does the student answer the question set?
- How well organised is it? Is the paragraphing good?
- Is there an effective opening and conclusion?
- Is the tone appropriate, i.e. does it sound like a letter from a grandson to grandparents?
- How accurate is it? Look at:
  - the spelling
  - the use of full stops
  - the use of apostrophes
  - the use of capital letters.
- Where there are mistakes or omissions, how would you correct them?

16 Crooked Lane,
Winsfield,
Cheshire

Dear gran and grandad

I can't believe that I am using a pen I also can't believe that you have not brought yourself into the modern world yet and got a computer so you can e-mail me and I don't have to write so much. How are you both? It seems like an eternity since the last time I saw you. The last time was at Sue and Dave's wedding me and the family are fine Andrew has Just started junior school and Sarah is halfway through primary school.

I am writting to you because you asked me for suggestions on what to get Andrew and Sarah for Christmas. I think that you should get them a Nintendo DS game each Because at the momment they are really into playing their Nintendo it seems that all they do is play on their Nintendo DS.

I also have a list of things that Andrew and Sarah might like I think that Andrew might also like things such as k-nex, lego and Mega blocks Because he really enjoys making things as well. I think that Sarah would like Barbie dolls and accessories.

But don't forget you can keep it simple I remember when I was young and you bought me some toy cars I really enjoyed them.

I hope that my letter has give you ideas on what to buy Sarah and Andrew. Oh and don't forget me! I hope I will see you sometime soon.

Toby.

106

Activity 4

Now complete your own informal letter.

Your grandparents live abroad and do not have a computer, but they really like receiving letters from you. Write a letter which will bring them up to date with what's going on where you live and which they will enjoy reading. (20 marks)

GradeStudio

Examiner tips

- Remember that accuracy is important, so take care with sentence structure, punctuation and spelling.
- Make sure you keep in mind who the letter is to, and the reason you are writing the letter.

Peer/Self-assessment

1 Check your answers to Activity 4.
- Did you set out your letter appropriately?
- Has it been paragraphed?
- Is there an introduction to the topic?
- Are the central paragraphs clearly organised into topics?
- Does it sound like a letter that would be sent to grandparents?

- Would they find it interesting?
- Are you happy with the level of clarity and accuracy?

2 Now try to grade your answer to Activity 4 using the mark scheme below. You will need to be careful and precise in your marking.

⬆ Moving up the grades

Content and organisation (13 marks)

A (10–13 marks)
- ▶ sophisticated understanding of purpose of task
- ▶ sustained awareness of reader
- ▶ coverage is well judged, and detailed
- ▶ points are convincingly developed
- ▶ paragraphs are used to enhance effect
- ▶ a sophisticated use of a range of stylistic devices
- ▶ appropriate and ambitious vocabulary.

C (7–9 marks)
- ▶ clear understanding of purpose of task
- ▶ clear awareness of audience
- ▶ good coverage
- ▶ ideas well shaped
- ▶ paragraphs used to structure writing
- ▶ style adapted to purpose/audience
- ▶ a good range of vocabulary.

D (4–6 marks)
- ▶ shows awareness of purpose of task
- ▶ shows awareness of audience
- ▶ satisfactory coverage
- ▶ logical ordering of paragraphs
- ▶ attempts to adapt style to purpose/audience
- ▶ some range in vocabulary used.

Sentence structure, punctuation and spelling (7 marks)

A (6–7 marks)
- ▶ effective variation of sentence structures
- ▶ sophisticated use of a range of sentences to achieve effect
- ▶ punctuation is accurate and used confidently
- ▶ virtually all spelling is correct
- ▶ tenses are fully under control.

C (4–5 marks)
- ▶ a good range of sentences is used to achieve effects
- ▶ a range of punctuation is used accurately
- ▶ most spelling of familiar and less familiar words is accurate
- ▶ control of tense and agreement is secure.

D (2–3 marks)
- ▶ sentences are varied
- ▶ some control of a range of punctuation
- ▶ spelling of commonly used words is usually accurate
- ▶ control of tense and agreement is generally secure.

My learning objectives ▼
- to learn about approaches to writing formal letters
- to understand the key differences between formal and informal letters.

Writing a formal letter

A formal letter is quite different from an informal letter. It has a different layout, audience, purpose and tone.

Activity 1

1 Make a list of occasions when you might need to write a formal letter.
2 How might a formal letter differ from an informal letter? Use your list and the notes below to help you. Create a table to show the similarities and differences between formal and informal letters.

Audience	In this type of letter you will be writing to a person you may not know personally or who you know in a more formal way. It might be a potential employer, a council official, a newspaper editor or a headteacher. This will clearly make a difference to the way in which you write the letter. The language and tone will be quite different from the chatty style of the letters we have looked at so far. Most letters of this type take a fairly serious approach.
Purpose	This could be to apply for a job, to give your view on an issue of concern to you, to complain etc. Whatever its purpose, it is important that your letter uses an appropriate tone. If you are writing a job application, you will want to impress; if you are writing on an issue of concern to you, you may, of course, express those views strongly and forcefully, but you should always be polite.
Format	This is different from the format of an informal letter. Again, you will include your address and the date, but this time you will also include the address of the recipient (the person you are writing to). (In the exam you may be given the address, but if not, you should make one up). The salutation will, in this case, be more formal, e.g. 'Dear Mr Asson' or 'Dear Sir/Madam' if you do not know the name of the person. The closure if you do not know the person's name will be 'Yours faithfully'. If you started the letter 'Dear Mrs Baker', then the letter should end 'Yours sincerely'.
Content	The question will tell you what the content should be, but whatever the topic, you must plan your letter. Think about your opening paragraph and then about the central points and how you intend to express them. Arguing or putting across your points logically is important and strengthens your case. Put yourself in the position of the recipient. The organisation will be similar to that suggested for the informal letter: • a fairly brief opening paragraph in which you outline/introduce your reason for writing • three or four central paragraphs in which you put your case • a final paragraph that rounds off the letter.

Let's look at how a formal letter might be set out.

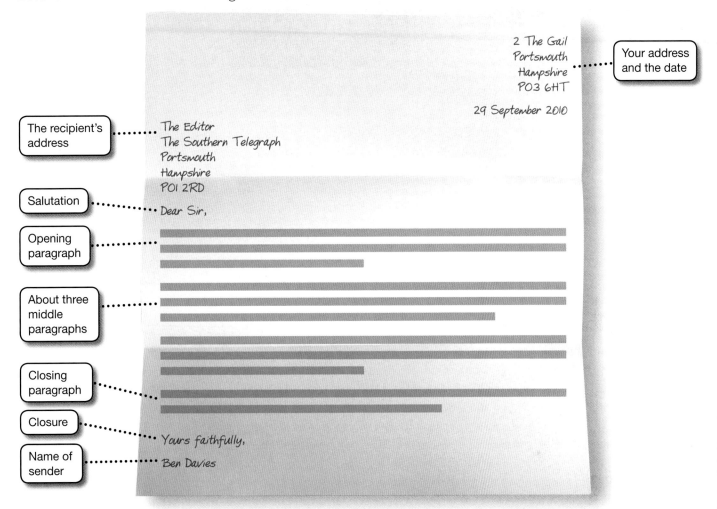

2 The Gail
Portsmouth
Hampshire
PO3 6HT

Your address and the date

29 September 2010

The recipient's address

The Editor
The Southern Telegraph
Portsmouth
Hampshire
POI 2RD

Salutation

Dear Sir,

Opening paragraph

About three middle paragraphs

Closing paragraph

Closure

Yours faithfully,

Name of sender

Ben Davies

Activity 2

1   A ban on smoking in public places has been introduced in England and Wales, and you are going to write a letter to your local newspaper giving your views on the subject.

    With a partner:
    - show how you would set out the letter
    - plan your opening paragraph
    - next, think about your honestly held views on the subject of smoking in public places and include two or three substantial points you can make for or against. These will be dealt with in your central paragraphs, i.e. one for each paragraph
    - plan your concluding paragraph which will round off the letter.

2   Now, on your own, using your plan, write the full version of the letter.

3   Finally, compare your letter with the letters in GradeStudio on pages 110–113. What could you do to improve it?

GradeStudio

Examiner tips

- When writing a formal letter, make sure it is suitable for the person(s) reading it. The tone will be different from a letter to a close friend. Bear in mind:
  - Purpose: why am I writing this piece?
  - Audience: who is it written for?
  - Format: how should my work be set out?
- Remember, if you do not know the name of the person you are writing to, the closure will be 'Yours faithfully'. If you do know the name of the person, it will be 'Yours sincerely'.

GradeStudio

Here are two formal letters written by students in response to the exam question below. Read the letters together with the examiner comments, then check what you have learnt and try putting it into practice.

A ban on smoking in public places has been introduced in England and Wales.

Write a letter to your local newspaper giving your views on the subject. You should write one to two pages in your answer book. (20 marks)

D grade answer

Student 1

Dear Sir/Madam,

I am writing to give my views on the smoking ban in public places in England and Wales.
I think it was about time the government got their act together and passed this law, it is a very long time overdue.
Before the law was introduced, I would have to sit in my local bar breathing second hand smoke from the gentleman in front of me, which I must say was truly **dissrespetful**.
I think smoking was a disgusting **habbit** in the first place and should never have taken off like it did. The ban has come as a great relief to the community, especially for the likes of my family who also used to have to breathe in other **peoples** smoke. Eating your food at a restaurant and **inhailing** smoke at the same time is not the most pleasant thing in the world, so **im** glad the government have finally put a stop to this.
Also, in addition to this law I think the government should take the situation a bit further and remove all branding from **ciggerette** boxes. In my opinion the way forward is to keep pushing restrictions on smoking until there are few smokers left. My reasons for this are because I think it is very unfair that little children **whos** parents decide to smoke have to inflict it on their small children. Nicotine is an extremely addictive substance and I think **its** cruel that there are people out there addicted to it and are harming their bodies. I think more should be done to help smokers off this dreadful substance
Yours **sincearly**,
David Morgan.

Examiner comment

There are good and not so good things about this piece of work. There is some format awareness and the student answers the set question. The letter has an introduction and is paragraphed. It expresses a strong point of view and some good vocabulary is used. However, there are no addresses and the closure is wrong.

Organisation is loose, suggesting lack of planning, and there is no real conclusion. Spelling is not very secure and there are other errors (indicated in bold) which will cost marks. The letter could be more persuasive rather than rant-like, which it is at times.

This is a D response. It was awarded a mark of 6/13 for content and organisation and 3/7 for sentence structure, punctuation and spelling. With a bit more care and attention to detail, a C grade could be achieved.

Student 2

3 Sophia Gardens,
Swansea
SA61 4HK

8th June 2010

The Editor,
'Swansea Post',
Market Street,
Swansea.

Dear Sir,

I am a man of habit, so when the smoking ban came into place i was so shocked I had to light a **ciggarrete**. I work hard all day and at the end of that day I feel it is my right, as I serve this country well, to go to the local, have a pint of ale and a good cigarette. It is against my human rights to have to go outside, banished from the warm fireside like a dog is banished from the house after raiding the bin, and have my well earned, well earned **ciggarette**. I don't see how some smoke free toffs can come into our locals and say that what we have been doing for years is damaging people's health. Codswallop! The locals and I are on twenty a day for twenty five years and apart from a little cough, I have never felt better.

Them ones in Westminster say that cigarettes cause cancer and disease, I say better die of that than a heart attack caused by stress.

Now my wife seems to agree with this smoking ban; she says that she couldn't go into the local because the smoke made her feel sick and she wouldn't take the children in there so now there's a smoking ban she's in there all the time! It's ruined my personal time because now she's always nagging me about being too loud or drinking too much; I used to go there to get away from the nagging, but now those lefty politicians have taken that away.

I feel that since this smoking ban the local has not felt the same; it has ruined the traditional pub and now there are women and families in it. Where am I supposed to go now to have a laugh with the lads? Every time I say I'm going to the Nag's Head the wife follows.

I say that we repeal this smoking ban and get back our human right to do what we want where we want and not have the wife to nag us.

Yours sincerely,
Carl S Burg

Examiner comment

The layout is good apart from the closure ('Yours sincerely') which is incorrect. The letter starts quite effectively and is organised in paragraphs. There is a conclusion. The student has decided to take on the role of the disgruntled husband and is quite successful in sustaining the character. The writing is mostly accurate but he can't decide on the correct spelling of 'cigarette' (in bold) and there is a little awkwardness as he strives for effect. This letter was awarded a high B grade: 11/13 for content and organisation; 4/7 for sentence structure, punctuation and spelling.

GradeStudio

Here is another formal letter written by a student in response to the exam question below. Read the letter together with the examiner comment, then check what you have learnt and try putting it into practice.

A ban on smoking in public places has been introduced in England and Wales.

Write a letter to your local newspaper giving your views on the subject. You should write one to two pages in your answer book. (20 marks)

A grade answer

Student 3

18 Ashford Street
Oxford
OX19 3NU

22 December 2010

Health supplement
The Oxford Monthly
Oxford
OX1

Dear Sir,

I am writing to express my views about the recent ban on smoking in public places in England and Wales. I am delighted.

I now feel that I can sit in a restaurant, café or bar in comfort. I no longer have to worry about the taste of smoke in my food or the smell of smoke on my clothes. I can even spend an evening out without having to wash both my hair and my pillow the next day because of the stale stench of smoke!

I hope that this new ban will encourage smokers to think about giving up so they don't have to spend hours outside in the cold while they smoke and more importantly they can improve their health and life expectancy.

One phenomena I have noticed which is a bit worrying, is that smoking could almost be seen as a more sociable option. When smokers huddle outside and share a light they strike up conversations that they may not have had if they were sitting inside with their non smoking friends. I hope that this doesn't become an excuse for people who do actually want to give up smoking for health reasons to continue to smoke.

I hope that this move towards better health for the whole nation will encourage the government to introduce other initiatives around areas such as diet and exercise to improve life for people in England and Wales.

Yours faithfully,

M E Johnson

Examiner comment

The letter is well set out and well organised. The opening paragraph makes clear the purpose of the letter and the isolated 'I am delighted' is there for effect and works well. The argument is quite 'narrow' but it is a valid, interesting if unusual point of view. The letter has an effective conclusion.

The tone throughout is appropriate and the letter is ambitiously and accurately written. Sentence control and spelling are secure. One error is the use of 'phenomena' rather than the singular 'phenomenon'.

Remember in transactional writing format, audience and purpose are central features. Here the student has a good grasp of all these aspects of this type of writing.

The mark awarded for this letter was 16 (10 + 6), so this answer would get a grade A.

Formal letters: how to go up the grades

To move up the grades some attention must be paid to layout features. You will need to plan what your approach is going to be and what you want to say: How will I introduce my letter? How can I best make what I have to say persuasive and convincing? How will I conclude so that my letter has impact and leaves the reader thinking about what I have said?

Say what you really think about the topic you have been asked to write about and don't be afraid to be controversial. Seeing both points of view in discussing a topic is fine, but the best letters usually have a clear and consistent viewpoint.

Remember that technical accuracy is important and impresses examiners, but don't be afraid to be ambitious with sentence structures and choice of words.

Putting it into practice

Discuss with a classmate what you have learnt in this section. Think about:
- the way in which a formal letter is set out and organised
- how it is different from an informal letter
- the different approaches you could take in a letter on a subject such as smoking or raising the driving age to 20.

In the future

- Learn and use the features of a formal letter.
- Always proofread your letters for sentence structure, punctuation and spelling.
- Make sure you know how to use and spell 'Yours sincerely' and 'Yours faithfully'.

My learning objectives ▼
- to practise using key features of a formal letter
- to develop a secure approach to writing a formal letter.

Exam practice and assessment

Read the formal letter below, in response to a question set in the exam.

A proposal has been made to hold a motorcycle race in your area. Write a letter to the local newspaper, giving your views on this proposal. (20 marks)

Dear Editor,

I am writing to express my total support for the proposed motorcycle race on the roads in and around Manchester. I cannot see why anybody would object to this proposal.

There have been races on the roads for runners, including Usain Bolt, so why should motorcyclists not get the same chance? I appreciate that not everybody is interested in this sport, but for those that are, this would be a fantastic opportunity to see some of their favourite riders.

As far as safety is concerned, the only people who face risks are those that choose to take them. I am sure that the city council will do everything they can to make the event both safe and enjoyable.

I resent negative people who complain about the noise. I believe that they should see this as an excuse to get away for the day. If it is quiet they seek, they could visit one of Manchester's lovely parks, far from the noise. You never know, they might just enjoy themselves for a change.

Financially, this event would be great. Fans and riders would come from all over Britain, or even the world, bringing money with them. If Manchester made a real effort to welcome and impress them, these people could return to give us business time and time again. Hotels, restaurants and tourist attractions would all see huge profits.

Personally, I can't wait. I love the excitement, the racers and the thrilling rush of adrenaline. If Manchester were to be invaded by an army of bikers, I would gladly surrender!

For all of these reasons, I strongly believe that this proposal should be encouraged. It would simply be cruel to deny the women of Manchester an army of bikers.

       Yours faithfully,

       Ruth Ross

Activity 3

This letter was awarded an **A*** grade in the examination (12/13 for content and organisation and 7/7 for sentence structure, punctuation and spelling). Note that the real version of the letter contained the writer's and recipient's address and the date.
Use the questions below to explain why this was given such a high mark.

- How has the letter been organised?
- How effective are the introduction and conclusion?
- What are the features of the central paragraphs? How persuasive and lively are they?
- How accurate is the writing? Look at the spelling of familiar and less familiar words. For example, 'business' is often misspelt and 'adrenaline' isn't easy.
- How effective is use of apostrophes, question marks and commas?
- Look also at the way in which sentences have been constructed. Is there variety in sentence length and type?
- If you were a newspaper editor, would you print this letter? Explain why.

Activity 4

Now complete your own formal letter using the following question set in the exam.

A TV magazine has invited readers to give their views on the standard of programmes on television. The magazine is offering a cash prize for the best response. Write your letter. (20 marks)

GradeStudio

Examiner tips

Remember:
- your address
- the recipient's address
- the date
- the salutation
- Does the opening paragraph introduce the topic?
- How well do the middle paragraphs make points clearly and effectively?
- Is the concluding paragraph effective?
- Have you signed off effectively?

Peer/Self-assessment

1 Check your answer to Activity 4.
- Did you set out your letter appropriately?
- Has it been paragraphed?
- Is there an introduction to the topic?
- Are the central paragraphs clearly organised into topics?

- Does it sound like a letter that would be printed in a magazine?
- Does it express views clearly?
- Are you happy with the level of clarity and accuracy?

2 Now try to grade your answer to Activity 4 using the mark scheme below. You will need to be careful and precise in your marking.

Moving up the grades

Content and organisation (13 marks)

A (10–13 marks)
- sophisticated understanding of purpose of task
- sustained awareness of reader
- coverage is well judged, and detailed
- points are convincingly developed
- paragraphs are used to enhance effect
- sophisticated use of a range of stylistic devices
- appropriate and ambitious vocabulary.

C (7–9 marks)
- clear understanding of purpose of task
- clear awareness of audience
- good coverage
- ideas well shaped
- paragraphs used to structure writing
- style adapted to purpose/audience
- a good range of vocabulary.

D (4–6 marks)
- shows awareness of purpose of task
- shows awareness of audience
- satisfactory coverage
- logical ordering of paragraphs
- attempts to adapt style to purpose/audience
- some range in vocabulary used.

Sentence structure, punctuation and spelling (7 marks)

A (6–7 marks)
- effective variation of sentence structures
- sophisticated use of a range of sentences to achieve effect
- punctuation is accurate and used confidently
- virtually all spelling is correct
- tenses are fully under control.

C (4–5 marks)
- a good range of sentences is used to achieve effects
- a range of punctuation is used accurately
- most spelling of familiar and less familiar words is accurate
- control of tense and agreement is secure.

D (2–3 marks)
- sentences are varied
- some control of a range of punctuation
- spelling of commonly used words is usually accurate
- control of tense and agreement is generally secure.

Writing a report

My learning objectives ▼
- to understand the nature of a report
- to learn how to plan, organise and complete such a report.

A report is intended to give information/advice to a person or persons so that what is said can be considered and, perhaps, acted upon.

Activity 1

What kinds of reports have you read or written? You have all received school reports.

Read through the notes below and share what you know about the different audiences and purposes for reports. Create a checklist that could be used by someone starting to write a report. Try to include all of the key features of a report in your checklist.

Purpose	The purpose of a report is to inform, advise or persuade a person or a group of people. It is normally written after something has been researched/investigated/thought about, for example the provision of public transport in an area. It gives up-to-date information to those who need it and can act upon it.
Format	There will be a clear and uncomplicated format so that the points raised are presented clearly to the reader(s). There will be a main heading and probably sub-headings, since the report is likely to consider different aspects of the subject. The clear separation of these points will help the reader(s) and will give shape and organisation to the work.
Audience	Most reports are written in a formal manner, though to a certain extent this can depend on who they are for. This might be your local council, your headteacher or your school council. The stated audience will, of course, help you to decide how the report is to be written. It will be more formal for the local council than for your fellow students, but even in this case there will be some formality.
Tone	This will be respectful, but that does not mean that you cannot put your views strongly. Making your points so that there can be no misunderstanding is not the same as being rude. Your points should be based on evidence and should be clearly made.

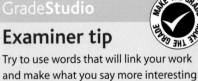

GradeStudio

Examiner tip

Try to use words that will link your work and make what you say more interesting – such as 'However', 'Importantly', 'Equally', 'At the same time'.

Read the example opposite of a report written in the exam. The student was asked to write a report for the school council on ways in which energy can be saved in his/her school/college.

Our Carbon Footprint

The Problem

At the end of year 08/09 the school had spent over £1000, yes, £1000 on electricity. This is a 40% increase on the previous year. Now, not only is this extremely expensive it's terrible for our planet. Our carbon footprint is way too big for our boots.

The Main Causes

Electricity is wasted around the school constantly. There are always computers left on even overnight. Interactive whiteboards, light bulbs, photocopiers – you name it and it is always left on. Even the eco club managed to leave the light on after last week's meeting. It may seem to some that one light bulb left on doesn't exactly cost much but adding all the lights in the school together gets us to a much higher total. The cost could accumulate to hundreds of pounds from light bulbs alone. As a school council and as a school we need to consider the polar bears.

But it's not only the polar bears we need to worry about. Think of yourselves. £1000 a year? That could be spent on books, school trips, sports equipment – the list is a long one. We are costing our education money.

The Solution

My ideas on how to save energy around the school are firstly (and most obviously) turn it off. If we are leaving a room, turn the light off. If we have finished on a computer, turn it off. Simple actions like these can save our school big sums of money. Secondly, perhaps the school council could persuade the headteacher to use energy saving light bulbs instead of regular ones. Perhaps a designated person each day could check rooms at the end of the day and turn off anything that doesn't need to be on.

As you can see fellow pupils the solution is simple and it lies in our own hands.

Examiner comment

The student has done what was asked for and her writing is focused, throughout, on the school. An effective heading and sub-headings have been used; there is a clear introduction, followed by an explanation of the problem. Logically, the student then moves on to solutions/recommendations. She shows awareness of her audience throughout.

Activity 2

Write your own report, using the exam question and the notes below to help you. Then compare your report with the one in GradeStudio on pages 118–119. How might you improve your report?

As secretary of your youth club, you have been asked to write a report on facilities for young children and teenagers in your area. Write what you would say. (20 marks)

Planning and writing your report

1 Make sure you understand exactly what you are being asked to do. Ask yourself:
   - What is the report about?
   - Who is it for?
2 Think of an appropriate heading. It can be straightforward or, if a good idea strikes you, catchy.
3 Under your first sub-heading, 'Introduction', briefly explain the background and purpose of your report.
4 Think of the areas you want to cover and choose sub-headings. You will probably only need three or four of these.
5 Under your heading 'Conclusion', briefly draw together your findings and make recommendations. Remember to be sensible and realistic if you want your report to be seriously considered. This is your last chance to influence the reader(s) of the report.

GradeStudio

Here is a report from a student in response to the exam question below. Read the report together with the examiner comments, then check what you have learnt and try putting it into practice.

As secretary of your youth club, you have been asked to write a report on facilities for young children and teenagers in your area. Write what you would say. (20 marks)

A grade answer

Student 1

<u>Bridport's facilities for young children and teenagers</u>

<u>Introduction</u>

As secretary of the local youth club I have compiled a report on the local facilities for teenagers and young children. I have compiled data through talking with fellow teenagers living in the area and this is an overview of my findings and possible solutions.

<u>Findings</u>

After speaking with various teenagers I have found the following things:

1 Teenagers feel that there isn't anywhere they can go with **there** friends unless they socialise where there are too many younger children e.g. at the youth club where there are 'too many primary school children shouting and screaming'.

2 Also those who do go to the youth centre find it increasingly dull and in desperate need of modernisation.

3 Furthermore the skate park and football fields are always crowded with 'intimidating individuals' and the feeling is that they are unapproachable, especially to girls and females generally who dislike the damaged and littered area.

4 The skate park is 'too far off the beaten track' and is outside the town so too far away from other people.

5 There aren't any clubs where teenagers and younger adults can meet up to socialise.

6 There is no sports hall where parties and other events can be held.

<u>Possible Solutions</u>

The problem about the youth club would be solved by simply refurbishing the centre and making it more accessible to people of our age. My solution to the other problem concerning our youth centre would be to dedicate certain days of the week and events exclusively to the teenage community.

As in the nearby town of Dorchester, I would suggest that a new more central skate park is created because as has been proved there it encourages co-operation, bonding and friendship as well as a fun environment to enjoy. This could also solve the problem of the park being too far off the beaten path whilst also discouraging the poor behaviour some individuals feel they can get away with because they are too far away from authoritative figures.

Older teenagers have had to travel as far as Sidmouth to go to clubs for younger people and this has meant that they have had an awful lot of trouble getting to and from this location. A solution could be to invest some money in having a council owned building so that they can go to somewhere closer and it could also be a significant money earner too.

Furthermore a newly developed sports and leisure centre would be a perfect solution and benefit all ages of the local community.

In conclusion I would like to thank you on behalf of all teenagers and adolescents in our area for letting our voice be heard amongst those who can make a real difference for us. I hope you will take all my findings into consideration because they will surely improve the facilities in the area for everyone.

Examiner summary

Remember that the mark out of 20 is divided between content and organisation (13) and sentence structure, punctuation and spelling (7).

Content and organisation
The report is detailed and well set out with clear headings and the writer uses a variety of presentational features, e.g. the numbering of the Findings. The tone is appropriate and the Findings are closely linked to the Possible Solutions section, though the 'clubs for younger people' is left a little vague. It is quietly persuasive and effectively concluded.

Sentence structure, punctuation and spelling
The report is clearly and accurately written throughout with just the odd error – '**there** friends'. There is ambition in the choice of words and a good range of vocabulary. There is security and variety in sentence construction and also an attempt to link points – 'Also', 'Furthermore', etc. Note the effective use of quotation.

Grade A (11/13 for content and organisation, 6/7 for sentence structure, punctuation, spelling).

Reports: how to go up the grades

- Read the question carefully.
- Ask yourself 'What is the purpose of this report?'
- Pay careful attention to audience.
- Use a main heading and sub headings.
- Introduce and conclude your report.
- Do your best to write accurately and effectively.

Putting it into practice

Discuss with a classmate what you have learnt in this section. Think about:
- the way in which a report is set out and organised
- what the purpose of the report is.

In the future
- Learn and use the features of a report.
- Always proofread your report for sentence structure, punctuation and spelling.
- Practise the skills you need to improve.

My learning objectives ▼

- to practise using key features of a report
- to develop a secure approach to writing a report.

Exam practice and assessment

Read the report below, written in response to a question set in the exam.

As secretary of your youth club, you have been asked to write a report on facilities for young children and teenagers in your area. Write what you would say. (20 marks)

Task: Local facilities for teenagers in Launceston and how they can be improved.

Background: To carry out the report I, as secretary to my local youth club, conducted a questionnaire to one hundred teenagers aged between thirteen and seventeen in my local area.

Problems

Whilst carrying out this report I found out that a shocking 69% of the teenagers that we surveyed thought that the facilities that we surveyed were very poor. They feel that despite the fact that there are a reasonable amount of physical activities, the availability ceases to exist due to the fact that they are snapped up on the day because there are only 12 places available. Also many teenagers used to enjoy relaxing in the town green. However it has grown over into a despicable state which could really be impossible for anyone to relax in. The cost of tickets to sail on the boating lake is extortionate meaning that no one is able to use it and a perfectly good lake is being wasted.

Recommendations

I recommend that as the council you provide teenagers with more recreational activities. For example tennis courts or a decent town green. Also I feel that you should employ more people to help out at after school clubs so that more people can take part.

Activity 1

This report was awarded a **C** grade in the exam (7/13 for content and organisation and 4/7 for sentence structure, punctuation and spelling), but it would not be difficult to improve the grade/mark awarded.

Use the questions below to suggest ways to improve the report.
- Does the writer make it clear what the report is about?
- Does he provide some background information?
- Are the problems clearly outlined and presented in an effective way?
- Do the recommendations tie in with what are seen as the problems?
- Is the tone of the report what you would expect?
- Is there clarity throughout?
- How accurate is the sentence structure, punctuation and spelling? How would you correct any mistakes?

Activity 2

Now complete your own report in response to the exam question below.

Write a report for your headteacher/principal about the ways in which your school/college prepares you for the world outside school/college. You may consider both the positive and the negative aspects. Remember the importance of format, audience and purpose. (20 marks)

GradeStudio

Examiner tip

In writing reports, many students say they have conducted a survey and give a string of statistics. Some of these are clearly absurd, making their report unconvincing. Avoid this approach.

Peer/Self-assessment

1 Check your answers to Activity 2.
- Did you set out your report in an effective manner?
- Did you pay careful attention throughout to your audience, i.e. the headteacher/principal?
- Was the tone used throughout appropriate, i.e. formal and respectful?
- Was what you said constructive and likely to be acted upon?

- Was your report sufficiently detailed but at the same point focused on the activity in hand?
- Did you ensure there was a high level of accuracy in your writing?

2 Now try to grade your answer to Activity 2 using the mark scheme below. You will need to be careful and precise in your marking.

⬆ Moving up the grades

Content and organisation (13 marks)

A (10–13 marks)
- sophisticated understanding of purpose of task
- sustained awareness of reader
- coverage is well judged, and detailed
- points are convincingly developed
- paragraphs are used to enhance effect
- a sophisticated use of a range of stylistic devices
- appropriate and ambitious vocabulary.

C (7–9 marks)
- clear understanding of purpose of task
- clear awareness of audience
- good coverage
- ideas well shaped
- paragraphs used to structure writing
- style adapted to purpose/audience
- a good range of vocabulary.

D (4–6 marks)
- shows awareness of purpose of task
- shows awareness of audience
- satisfactory coverage
- logical ordering of paragraphs
- attempts to adapt style to purpose/audience
- some range in vocabulary used.

Sentence structure, punctuation and spelling (7 marks)

A (6–7 marks)
- effective variation of sentence structures
- sophisticated use of a range of sentences to achieve effect
- punctuation is accurate and used confidently
- virtually all spelling is correct
- tenses are fully under control.

C (4–5 marks)
- a good range of sentences is used to achieve effects
- a range of punctuation is used accurately
- most spelling of familiar and less familiar words is accurate
- control of tense and agreement is secure.

D (2–3 marks)
- sentences are varied
- some control of a range of punctuation
- spelling of commonly used words is usually accurate
- control of tense and agreement is generally secure.

Writing articles for magazines and newspapers

My learning objectives ▼
- to understand the features of an article
- to understand what makes an article effective.

Articles are mostly written for newspapers and magazines. If you are asked to write one, it is vital that you fully understand its purpose, audience and format.

Activity 1

Collect some newspapers and magazines and look at the different sorts of articles. Discuss with a partner the things that are similar or different. Use the notes below to guide your thinking.

Purpose	In most cases a magazine or newspaper article is written to inform, persuade and entertain. The exact emphasis is up to the writer, e.g. their main aim may be to tell the reader what has happened, to get readers thinking, or to amuse them, or it could be a combination of these. Whatever the precise aim, most articles need to be written in a lively style and contain interesting facts and probably opinions. You may hold any opinion you like, but what you have to say should be convincingly and clearly argued.
Audience	The style and tone will be adapted to suit the audience – an article written for a school or teenage magazine will sound different from one for a national or local newspaper. If you are asked, in the exam, to write an article, you will be told who it is for and where it will appear.
Format	This is uncomplicated. An article usually has a main heading that makes it clear what the article is about, though there is room to use the heading to attract the reader's attention with a pun or a bit of ambiguity, e.g. 'Hitting the bottle' was an article about hair-dye kits. The use of paragraphs is important. They will give a bit of shape and organisation to your article. There is no need, in the examination, to use columns as in magazines and newspapers, but you can if you wish. Your name, as the writer, should appear beneath the heading.

What makes a good article?

An effective article is carefully written, interests and informs its readers, makes them think and causes them to react. There are a number of ways you can achieve this.

▶ Choose a subject that is interesting and topical. Subjects that are topics of conversation now will be more appealing than dated ones.

▶ Select what you want to say carefully. You cannot hope to cover everything, for example, if you are writing an article about a visit to a major city like Manchester or New York.

▶ Use a style and devices that will give the article a lively feel, but remember that a lot will depend on the publication and the audience. You may decide that it is appropriate to be informal and chatty, to use questions to draw the audience in, to repeat a word or phrase for effect, to use irony or sarcasm, to make bold statements or to be controversial in order to shock, etc.

▶ Organise your material in a purposeful way with:
  ▶ a catchy heading
  ▶ an introduction that engages the reader
  ▶ three or four central paragraphs
  ▶ a short but telling conclusion.

Activity 2

Your local newspaper is running a series of articles on subjects of interest to teenagers. You have been asked to contribute an article on: 'Mobile phones, a blessing or a curse?' Before you write your article, read the outline below and the examiner comments, and think carefully about the following:

- the purpose of your article
- the intended audience
- a suitable heading (try to make it catchy)
- an introduction that will draw the readers in
- how you will organise your work
- how many paragraphs you will use and what will go in them
- an effective rounding-off (conclusion).

> This article has a neat, engaging heading.

Mobile Madness or Maybe Not

By Dominic Asson

The mobile phone is certainly one of the most popular inventions ever. Over the last decade it has changed from a thing the size of a brick to something which slips comfortably into a pocket.

Almost all of us have one. Why?

Teenagers are particularly fond of them.

Of course, there are other groups that cannot manage without them.

That is not to say that they are without their drawbacks.

So, good or evil, blessing or curse?

> The introductory paragraph is short and sharp.

> First of four middle paragraphs; these are planned, with an attempt to link them.

> Second paragraph.

> Third paragraph.

> Fourth paragraph.

> The conclusion is going to draw the points together and give a final opinion.

GradeStudio

Examiner tips

Articles can be written on many subjects in a range of publications. Newspapers and magazines often publish articles on places that reporters have visited. The purpose is to give an honest view which may be flattering or very critical or a mixture of the two. The writer will try hard to engage your interest. Ask yourself:

- What is the writer trying to do?
- Does s/he succeed?
- What methods are used to achieve his/her purpose?
- How well written is it?

GradeStudio

Here are two student articles for a teenage magazine in response to the exam question below, on the topic 'Life Since Becoming a Teenager'. Read the articles together with the examiner comments, then check what you have learnt and try putting it into practice.

Write an informative and entertaining article about being a teenager. (20 marks)

Student 1

Tantrums, Texting and Teens

Being a teen are the greatest years of a person's life. Or are they? Your reporter gives her view.

I'm now 15 years old and am halfway through my teenage years. It's safe to say, I kinda like it.

I'm now given a say in what time I go to bed – usually 11, but that's a secret. I can go out wearing what I want, within reason – obviously no leather micro-minis or see through crop tops with a face full of make-up. I'm not that free! I can also go to places further away with my mates without my parents having to take me. Even got the train to Manchester the other week!

Although all these reasons sound brilliant about being a teen, it also has **it's downsides**.

I'm given more responsibility which can be great, **when going** out, but I'm now talking about a different sort of responsibility.

For example, all the coursework and homework you are given. It is your responsibility to get it done. And as you get older, you gradually get more and more. I struggle to keep up but of course it helps with your parents nagging you though I hate it when they do. It's difficult sometimes but you have to remember they're only trying to help. Anyway, I think I must leave you now as I have some coursework to complete and some streets to wander. But if you think about it being a teen isn't half as bad as it's made out to be.

Examiner comment

This student does what she has been asked to do, i.e. write an entertaining and lively article. The tone of the piece is appropriate and her voice comes through very effectively.

To improve, she needs to maintain the pleasant tone but develop the answer – for example, a little more about life outside school, relationships with parents, what being a 15-year-old in school entails. It would also be necessary to get rid of the touch of awkwardness that appears from time to time – for example where she says 'when going'. Errors, too, should be eliminated – for example, 'it's downsides'.

Grade C (8/13 for content and organisation; 4/7 for sentence structure, punctuation and spelling).

Articles: how to go up the grades

- Think carefully about the subject you have been asked to write about.
- The audience will be indicated in the question, e.g. 'for teenage readers'. Make sure you write for that audience.
- The tone you will need to adopt should now be clear. If the piece is for your peer group it will sound different from an article intended for adults.
- Try to make it lively and interesting, e.g. by using humour, but don't force this.
- Make sure that your writing is accurate. Remember there is a difference between writing informally and writing sloppily.
- Check your work.

Student 2

Changes? Yeah Right!

How much has my life changed since my sixteenth birthday? If I really think about it, not much.

Sure, when I was twelve I imagined myself spending my teenage years in a frenzy of hormones and anger, turning into a violent shadow of my former self. I thought that I would be so hormone-crazed that I would not remember how much I used to love my family, and would spend my teen years (after sixteen of course) enveloped in the opposite sex. Fortunately, this seems not to be the case.

Instead, as a teenager I am faced with different problems. All the important exams that we teenagers have to take, such as GCSEs, give us a huge amount of responsibility for our futures, when we barely know that we even want to grow up.

We are faced with the sudden need to defend ourselves against the stereotype of a 'normal' teenager – ones who like slouching around in hoodies scaring old ladies – so that adults will give us more respect. We have to start taking responsibility for our actions, and, as many girls will tell you, we can no longer wander around in any old outfit – we have to dress and be 'cool'.

Thinking back to my pre teen years, it is almost laughable how immature I was. I would not say that I have suddenly gained the maturity needed to be an adult, but I would argue that teenagehood is a wake up call for us, making us remember that we can't do something stupid and expect people to say 'Isn't she adorable?' and then be taken under the wing of our parents.

Being a teenager is probably the hardest point in life. Too old to be cute, and considered by most adults too young to be taken seriously, we really are at the hardest point in life.

Teenagers get the worst rap in the press, and our work – at school – is scrutinised by more people in the country than any other age group. But think of all the good stuff. Sleepovers and shopping, mates and dates, teenagers can often live the social part of an adult's life without facing the responsibility and financial worry that most adults have to bear.

I would say that being a teenager is the best part of life. So enjoy your freedom while you can. Before you have to give it up and finish growing up. To teenagers!!!

Examiner comment

The response answers the question. It has a clear sense of purpose and audience and the tone is pleasant. It is interesting and honest. The length of the article is well judged. There is fluency in the writing and control/organisation are very good. Note the shaping of sentences. The work is almost entirely accurate. An examiner would have no difficulty in awarding work of this quality Grade A* (12–13/13 for content and organisation; 6–7/7 for sentence structure, punctuation and spelling).

Putting it into practice

Discuss with a classmate what you have learnt in this section. Think about:
- the features of articles and what makes them effective
- how articles are made interesting for their readers
- how articles are written with an audience in mind.

My learning objectives ▼

- to practise using key features of an article
- to develop a secure approach to writing an article.

Exam practice and assessment

In newspaper articles/magazines you will often see articles on places that have been visited by reporters. The purpose is to give an honest view which may be flattering or very critical or a mixture of the two. The writer will try hard to engage your interest. Read the article below, in response to the following exam question:

Write an article for a travel magazine based on a place you have visited and found interesting. (20 marks)

Hav'ana good time

First of all, Cuba. Everyone gets the pronunciation wrong so don't worry if you do first time. It's not 'Queue-ba' its 'Koo-ba'. 'Koo-ba' is the most unspoilt island in the Caribbean. The isolation which followed the revolution of 1958 meant that, for a long time, few visitors ever went there,

My first stop was the city of Havana and one of its most famous hotels – Hotel Nacional. The twin towered hotel has been visited by such diverse characters as Winston Churchill and Robert Plant. The downstairs bar has an interesting collection of photos of celebrities who have stayed there. The hotel fell on hard times but was renovated in the 1990s and is now one of the capital's best.

My first sightseeing trip was to the 'Catedral de la Habana' which dominates a delightful square in the heart of old Havana and is a striking and almost over elaborate building. The interior, by contrast, is simple and plain apart from the decorative altar. The cathedral is well worth a visit. One of its most interesting features is a coffin which is believed to hold the remains of Christopher Columbus. After leaving the cathedral I wandered a short way and found myself in a flea market held from Tuesday to Sunday. A wonderful sight with bright colours and the sound of Cuban music, there was a surprising amount of objects for sale – and most were hand made.

Another must see is the 'Museo de la Revolucion'. The building has been described as looking like a wedding cake. You either love it or loathe its over-the-topness. Impossible to view everything in one visit, there are items that should not be missed, including: Che Guevara's black beret, Fidel Castro's trousers and much more.

A memorable moment for me was taking a trip in a horse and cart. Like all Cubans the driver was a cheerful and chatty man. He showed us a garage full of 1950s cars in excellent condition. In addition, no visit would be complete without a short trip in a unique three seated yellow Cuban taxi. Possibly a little on the unsafe side with no seat belts and the risk of falling out, but a very unforgettable experience.

A highlight of my time in Havana was a visit to the 'Buena Vista Club', an assortment of musicians who played in the concert hall next to the Hotel Nacional.

After five exhilarating days in Havana I travelled to the Varadero Peninsula to stay in a beach hotel. This proved very relaxing with some special features, though it was not the same 'flavour' as the real Cuba. Having said that our hotel was ideal. With the beach on the doorstep and a bar in the pool, it's the perfect place to relax and enjoy the sun.

Cuba has left a lasting impression on me – the colours and sounds were so vivid. It was so fascinating to see a society which is so different from our own.

Activity 1

Although this is not the complete article, there is enough here to judge its quality. If you were the examiner, what mark would you award for this article? Remember that the mark of 20 is split between content and organisation (13) and sentence structure, punctuation and spelling (7). Use the mark scheme opposite to help your judgement.

Activity 2

Now write your own article, using this question set in the exam.

Write an article for a primary school newspaper in which you tell the Year 6 class what life is like in your secondary school. (20 marks)

GradeStudio

Examiner tip

In activities such as these, be honest and draw on your personal experience and observations.

Peer/Self-assessment

1 Check your answers to Activity 2.
- Did you set out your article appropriately?
- Is there a catchy heading?
- Has it been paragraphed?
- Does the introduction engage the reader?
- Are the central paragraphs clearly organised?
- Is the article rounded off with a short conclusion?
- Does it sound like a primary school newspaper article for Year 6?
- Are you happy with the level of clarity and accuracy?

2 Now try to grade your answer to Activity 2 using the mark scheme below. You will need to be careful and precise in your marking.

Moving up the grades

Content and organisation (13 marks)

A (10–13 marks)
- sophisticated understanding of purpose of task
- sustained awareness of reader
- coverage is well judged, and detailed
- points are convincingly developed
- paragraphs are used to enhance effect
- a sophisticated use of a range of stylistic devices
- appropriate and ambitious vocabulary.

C (7–9 marks)
- clear understanding of purpose of task
- clear awareness of audience
- good coverage
- ideas well shaped
- paragraphs used to structure writing
- style adapted to purpose/audience
- a good range of vocabulary.

D (4–6 marks)
- shows awareness of purpose of task
- shows awareness of audience
- satisfactory coverage
- logical ordering of paragraphs
- attempts to adapt style to purpose/audience
- some range in vocabulary used.

Sentence structure, punctuation and spelling (7 marks)

A (6–7 marks)
- effective variation of sentence structures
- sophisticated use of a range of sentences to achieve effect
- punctuation is accurate and used confidently
- virtually all spelling is correct
- tenses are fully under control.

C (4–5 marks)
- a good range of sentences is used to achieve effects
- a range of punctuation is used accurately
- most spelling of familiar and less familiar words is accurate
- control of tense and agreement is secure.

D (2–3 marks)
- sentences are varied
- some control of a range of punctuation
- spelling of commonly used words is usually accurate
- control of tense and agreement is generally secure.

My learning objectives ▼
- to understand what makes a leaflet a distinctive publication
- to understand how to make a leaflet effective.

Writing leaflets

Leaflets are all around you. You will find them in shops, hotels, tourist offices, doctors' surgeries, restaurants and so on. If asked to write a leaflet in the exam, you cannot be expected to produce the real thing, but you can show that you:

▶ understand their purpose

▶ can write for and engage an appropriate audience

▶ can adopt the right tone and style

▶ can use/indicate some of the format features.

Activity 1

Read the following notes, and the extract from the leaflet opposite.

1   What is the purpose of the leaflet? How do you know?
2   Who is the intended audience? How do you know?
3   What features suggest that this is a leaflet?
4   How is the information presented and is it easy to access?
5   How does the leaflet attempt to attract and persuade you? Look at its layout and organisation, the language used, the information provided and any other features you consider effective.

Purpose	Leaflets may be written to tell people things they may want or need to know. The government will issue leaflets to inform people about their entitlements, health issues (e.g. a flu epidemic, smoking, excessive drinking, obesity). Some of the most commonly seen leaflets advertise places to visit, such as theme parks, National Trust properties or castles.
Audience	The audience will vary: a leaflet on a paintballing facility will probably be aimed at younger people, while a leaflet advertising gardens will probably be targeted at adults. But remember that most leaflets such as those focused on a theme park or a holiday destination will seek to attract as wide an audience as possible.
Tone and style	These will reflect the intended audience, so a leaflet whose main audience is teenagers will be much less formal than one intended for older people. You would not expect a leaflet advertising a rollercoaster park to have the same tone as one about a stately home. It is vital, however, that any leaflet engages the interest of the intended reader.
Format	This will vary according to purpose. However, it should be organised in such a way that information is conveyed clearly and is easy to find. The title will immediately tell the reader what it is about and sub-headings/sections will clearly indicate the different subjects/interests covered.

The benefits of recycling food waste

 It gives you the opportunity to recycle more of your waste.

 Reduces the odour caused by rotting food waste by providing a special containment system and regular service.

 It reduces the amount of waste that has to be placed in landfill, which helps to cut down the cost of waste disposal.

 It reduces the amount of methane gas produced in landfill sites, which contributes to climate change.

Your larger bin is lockable, easy to carry and their design prevents access to the waste by scavenging animals such as foxes, cats, seagulls, dogs etc.

This scheme allows you to:

 Review your spending – could you save money on food once you are more aware of how much you throw away?

For practical advice on how to reduce food waste, visit www.lovefoodhatewaste.com

If you have any queries about this new collection please call our contact centre on

 Pembrokeshire County Council

01437 764551

www.pembrokeshire.gov.uk/wasteandrecycling

Activity 2

Create your own leaflet, thinking about all of the features looked at in Activity 1.

GradeStudio

Here is a leaflet written by a student in response to the exam question below. Read the leaflet together with the examiner comment, then check what you have learnt and try putting it into practice.

Write a leaflet to encourage people to give up smoking. (20 marks)

Student 1

Smoking – Time to butt out the Fag butt?
Thousands of people in the UK smoke. Thousands of people die each year from smoking related illnesses. So why do you smoke? You could be the next person to die. 'So what are the benefits from not smoking?' you ask. Well this leaflet is designed to convince you to get off the cigarettes.

Better Health
Have you noticed your nails going slightly yellow? Or maybe your constantly coughing? All of these are signs that the 200 chemicals in cigarettes are begining to effect and deteriorate your health. If you continue to smoke it is possible to get lung cancer, bronchitis and other respiratory illnesses. Gradually, your senses of taste and smell begin to deteriorate.

Strapped for Cash?
People can smoke as many as 40/50 cigarettes a day. If a pack of twenty costs £5 that's at least ten pounds a day (£3000 a year) on something that could kill you. That money could mean that a few of lifes luxuries could be yours. How about a holiday in the sun? Changing your old banger for a more modern vehicle? Treating your son/daughter to the latest i pod?

Smells Great Tastes Great
As mentioned under Health your senses of taste and smell deteriorate when you smoke. What a horrible world it would be if you couldn't taste your own roast dinner or couldn't smell the cake baking in the oven – all of that because of smoking. Is it really worth it?

Cleaner Home, Cleaner Life
As a smoker what does your house smell like or don't you notice anymore? If you don't visitors certainly will. And what about your children? You've surely heard of passive smoking and the damage it can do to innocent people who don't even smoke. What about your white ceilings that are now stained a dirty yellow making your place look grubby and adding to your decorating bill?

Fitness Test
So how fit are you? That hill you used to walk up without any trouble does that now present problems? And the 5 aside matches can you keep going right to the end or are you gasping for breath?

Examiner comment

The purpose of the activity is clearly understood and the piece has a good sense of audience and an effective tone. Good use is made of persuasive techniques (use of startling figures, uncomfortable facts, questions, repetition). Attention is paid to layout and the piece is quite accurately written. More could have been said under sub-headings, for example the final one. The leaflet ends abruptly and there is no concluding section. The work is not without errors such as 'begining', 'effect', 'lifes'. Word choices could have been better – for example, the overuse of 'deteriorate'. This response is a B grade: 8/13 for content and organisation and 5/7 for sentence structure, punctuation and spelling.

Grade**Studio**

Examiner tip

Some leaflets will be dominated by graphics, but in the exam you will be tested on your understanding of the question and the quality of your writing.

Leaflets: how to go up the grades

To move up the grades you need to:

- Understand the purpose of the leaflet you write.
- Think about the intended audience. This may be quite a specific group of people, e.g. primary school pupils or a wide range of people.
- Adopt a suitable tone for the specific leaflet, e.g. a leaflet on a health issue will be more serious than one trying to persuade you to visit an attraction.
- Set it out in a way that is helpful to the reader (i.e. using a heading, sub-headings) and include information required by the reader.
- Draw on your personal knowledge and experience where possible.
- Write at sufficient length but don't overdo it. Aim for about a page and a half.
- Write clearly and accurately.

Putting it into practice

- Think of a place you like visiting which you think people of your age would also enjoy.
- Plan a leaflet intended to persuade your peer group to go there.
- Think of a main heading and sub-headings.
- Remember that you are not required to use illustrations but you can indicate where they might be placed if you wish.
- Next, think of the methods of persuasion you will use.
- Ask a fellow student to look at your plan and give an opinion.

In the future

- Learn and use the features of a leaflet.
- Always proofread your report for sentence structure, punctuation and spelling.
- Practise the skills you need to improve.

My learning objectives ▼

- to practise using key features of a leaflet
- to develop a secure approach to writing a leaflet.

Exam practice and assessment

Read the leaflet below, in response to the following exam question.

Your local community wants to raise money to spend on local facilities. It has organised a fund-raising day and has asked you to write a leaflet to attract as many people as possible. Write your leaflet. (20 marks)

Leaflet

This year the Axe Valley community would like to set up several fund raising events to raise money to improve the quality of local facilities.
5 We would like to raise enough money to make facilities accessible to all ages.

What we are intending to do now!

We would like to improve the leisure facilities that are already in the Axe Valley. This includes
10 fitness and sports facilities, local organisations and clubs and general recreation areas. To begin with we intend to develop places such as the swimming pool and make it be more accessible for both younger and older children as we have
15 noticed that mainly the pool is dominated by middle aged and elderly people and we would like to feel that the pool is available for use by everybody. Another sports facility that we would develop is the sports centre as it is set
20 up so that only younger children can use it. We would also like to provide more equipment in recreation areas such as parks and football fields as they are painfully depleted.

What we are intending to do in the near future!

25 We want to raise enough money to be able to build a whole new building that can be used for recreational activities, sports activities, organisation's meetings and just simply 'hanging out'! We are not expecting to raise enough
30 money for this just with this fundraising event but it would be helpful if we could get some money towards it so every little helps.

When is the next fundraising event???

On the 27th July on the Church Green, we are having a small fair with lots of games 35 and stalls. As we are trying to raise money to improve facilities for all ages we will have interesting stalls for all ages. There will be ordinary stalls such as tombola, homemade cakes, books and jumble. The guides are also running 40 a stall to show that there are organisations that will benifit from our future plans. There will also be a stand where there will be more detailed information about what we want to do and also for you to give us more ideas about 45 what you, as the public, would like from us.

WE CAN'T DO THIS WITHOUT YOUR HELP; COME ALONG AND SUPPORT US ON THE 27TH OF JULY!!!

Activity 3

Using the mark scheme opposite and what you have learnt about leaflets, how successful do you think this leaflet is?

Activity 4

Now write your own leaflet, using the following exam question.

Write a leaflet to advertise a newly opened theme park intended to appeal to thrill-seekers of any age. (20 marks)

Peer/Self-assessment

1 Check your answers to Activity 4.
- Did you target thrill-seekers of any age?
- Did you write with a purpose – to inform and persuade?
- Did you organise and format your leaflet using headings and paragraphs?
- How accurate are your sentence structure, punctuation and spelling?

2 Now try to grade your answer to Activity 4 using the mark scheme below. You will need to be careful and precise in your marking.

 ## Moving up the grades

Content and organisation (13 marks)

A (10–13 marks)
- sophisticated understanding of purpose of task
- sustained awareness of reader
- coverage is well judged, and detailed
- points are convincingly developed
- paragraphs are used to enhance effect
- sophisticated use of a range of stylistic devices
- appropriate and ambitious vocabulary.

C (7–9 marks)
- clear understanding of purpose of task
- clear awareness of audience
- good coverage
- ideas well shaped
- paragraphs used to structure writing
- style adapted to purpose/audience
- good range of vocabulary.

D (4–6 marks)
- shows awareness of purpose of task
- shows awareness of audience
- satisfactory coverage
- logical ordering of paragraphs
- attempts to adapt style to purpose/audience
- some range in vocabulary used.

Sentence structure, punctuation and spelling (7 marks)

A (6–7 marks)
- effective variation of sentence structures
- sophisticated use of a range of sentences to achieve effect
- punctuation is accurate and used confidently
- virtually all spelling is correct
- tenses are fully under control.

C (4–5 marks)
- a good range of sentences is used to achieve effects
- a range of punctuation is used accurately
- most spelling of familiar and less familiar words is accurate
- control of tense and agreement is secure.

D (2–3 marks)
- sentences are varied
- some control of a range of punctuation
- spelling of commonly used words is usually accurate
- control of tense and agreement is generally secure.

My learning objectives ▼
- to explore what makes a good speech
- to learn how to construct a speech.

Writing a speech or talk

A speech or talk is an address to a group of people large or small. As part of your Speaking and Listening activities you may already have delivered one to your classmates or to a less familiar audience.

Activity 1

1 Think of speeches/talks you have listened to, e.g. from a visitor to your school, from your headteacher, from famous people on television. Which ones have you enjoyed and which ones haven't you?. Write down your reasons for your different reactions, then read the notes below.

2 Find a famous speech or two on the Internet, such as Abraham Lincoln's 'Gettysburg Address', Winston Churchill's 'We will fight them on the beaches', Martin Luther King's 'I have a dream', Nelson Mandela's 'An ideal for which I am prepared to die' or Earl Spencer's speech at Princess Diana's funeral. Write notes on what you think makes them effective. Look at:

- what is said
- how the arguments are developed
- the vocabulary: pick out words that are particularly effective
- the sentences: pick out some that are memorable and explain why
- the overall impact: why has this become a famous speech?

Writing a speech

If you are asked to write a speech in the exam, you will be informed of its intended audience and purpose.

Purpose	Speeches might be to give information, to explain/argue a point of view and perhaps, to persuade. The emphasis will be different depending on the precise circumstances. A politician's emphasis will be on persuasion, while a scientist might concentrate on giving information and raising issues.
Audience	In the exam this will be made clear to you; it is a vital piece of information. The content and style of a speech for younger children will be very different from a speech intended for the governing body of your school or a group of local business people.
Tone	This again will be influenced by audience and circumstances. If you are talking to your classmates, it may be less formal and more chatty than if you are addressing adults. If it is a contribution to a phone-in, it will probably be less formal.

1 Using the guidelines for planning and writing a speech below, write a speech in response to the following question set for the exam.

For your Speaking and Listening assessment for GCSE English, you have been asked to address your class on the topic 'Things I would happily put in Room 101'. Try to be entertaining and explain why you would want to get rid of the things you hate. (20 marks)

2 Compare your answer to those in GradeStudio on pages 136–137. Which one is your speech closest to? How could you improve your speech?

Planning and writing your speech

The following steps will help you to plan and write a speech.
You could learn this to help you plan and write speeches in the exam.

1 Open with a welcome/greeting to your audience. This will be brief and simple – 'Good morning, ladies and gentlemen' or 'Fellow classmates…'

2 Outline the subject of the speech: 'I intend to talk today about the size zero controversy that has filled our newspapers and television bulletins of late. My argument will be that this obsession with conforming to a certain look is very misguided.'

3 Make three or four key points (one for each paragraph) to support and develop your argument. Remember that it is vital to keep the attention of your audience, so your selection of points/evidence is very important. Your aim is to win over your audience to your point of view.

4 Write a conclusion that will have an impact on the audience and leave them with something to think about.

5 End with an acknowledgement of the audience, such as 'Thank you for listening so attentively.'

> **GradeStudio**
>
> **Examiner tip**
> You can inform and persuade in many different ways. The list on this page will help you.

The hallmark of a good speech is capturing and holding the attention of those listening. There are various things that will help you to do this:

▶ adopting the right tone

▶ using, but not overusing, rhetorical devices such as 'It is fair to say', 'I am sure you will agree', 'It is often claimed that…', 'Is it really the case that…'

▶ using humour: audiences like wit and like to be amused

▶ using repetition, e.g. 'Those who disagree with me … claim … they claim … they claim …'

▶ using statistics, but not bombarding the audience with them

▶ coming up with a memorable phrase of your own, or a quotation

▶ using anecdotes/personal experience

▶ being controversial.

GradeStudio

Here are two speeches written by students in response to the exam question below. Read the speeches together with the examiner comments, then check what you have learnt and try putting it into practice.

For your Speaking and Listening assessment for GCSE English, you have been asked to address your class on the topic 'Things I would happily put in Room 101'. Try to be entertaining and explain why you would want to get rid of the things you hate. (20 marks)

C grade answer

Student 1

The first thing I would put into Room 101, is the England football team. I'm no football fan or player but even an idiot could play better than them. All they do is pass backwards. They didn't even qualify for Euro 2008. I mean come on even Russia qualified! **Its** so cold there I bet they don't even **practice** for half the year as **their** snowed in. Secondly, me being a girl and all shall we say I may have an ulterior motive watching football. But no one on the England football team is remotely good looking! What's the point of having a football team who no one in their right mind would like to fancy! Why can't they look like the Brazilian team?

The second thing I would love to send to Room 101 is Katie Price and Peter Andre who at time of writing have split. So why send them? Firstly Katie is so full of herself and tries to control Pete. And Pete?... well Pete is a complete idiot for want of a better word! They are both completely fake. Their TV programmes are complete rubbish and are just to make them money, taking up valuable space for a programme people would love to watch

The third thing I would like to send to Room 101 is an item this time. Can you guess what it is? It is a cucumber that has been put in brine, vinegar or water and left to ferment. Now the first reason to send this to Room 101. They taste absolutely foul and make any normal person feel sick. Secondly their smell is atrocious. Pickle breath needs **to be rid of this world** so we can all **breath** normally again. Thirdly stupid restaurants like McDonalds put them in everything. If pickles **were rid of this world** I could finally enjoy my McDonalds without having to pick my burger apart.

My last item is again a person. I want to send Bruce Forsythe to Room 101, because he is potentially the most annoying person on this entire planet. His jokes are always lame and no one ever laughs at his jokes. I have never listened to anyone trying to be funny and **feel** so depressed. In addition he thinks he can sing and dance. All I can say to that is – no Bruce, you can't. Bruce, do us all some good, go to 101 and stop annoying us.

Examiner comment

The question clearly indicates the audience, explains the purpose of the activity and asks for a speech that is entertaining. The student has the audience in mind here, understands the purpose and makes every effort to be entertaining – there is a pleasantly informal tone and some attempt at humour. She is outspoken and provocative and what is said holds the reader's/listener's attention. The talk is quite fluently written.

There is, however, room for improvement. The student jumps straight into the task without acknowledging her audience. Perhaps she could address them to round off the speech, though there is a case for ending the way she does for dramatic effect. The links between paragraphs could be improved. There are errors and some examples of awkwardness, indicated in bold. Grade C (9–10/13 for content; 4/7 for sentence structure, punctuation and spelling).

Student 2

Okay, this is going to come off as extraordinarily snobbish, but more than anything else, I would put 'Sun' readers in Room 101 i.e. full-on red-top readers, who maybe grab an issue of the grubby tabloid every day of every week to see the latest Brangelina gossip masquerading as, as it once claimed in bold print on the cover, 'The Only Real News You'll Ever Need'. This from the same issue that proclaimed its knowledge of Pamela Anderson's sex life with bold relish and pride normally reserved for smug parents watching their pampered child win at sports day. And trust me: there is a special circle in Hell reserved for those who dare subscribe to the 'Sun'. Speaking of whom – smug parents; that unbearably smarmy group of people who every parents evening, every sports day...

Who watches the 'Apprentice'? As far as I can tell, there's a rather outnumbered minority who get a good kick one evening a week out of watching people who, by all rights should be under state care, pretend to have vast reservoirs of business acumen, chortling gaily at those hapless fools attempting to rebrand Shoreditch, or whatever. And then, there seems to be the vast majority of the British public – I'd imagine the same people who watch 'Big Brother' or think that Susan Boyle is a sensation, or read the 'Sun' for that matter who genuinely root for these people and their lamentable business skills...

I'm beginning to feel like one of those awful American stand up comics that you see in seedy downstairs bars in Manhattan – you know the kind I mean, 'arty' ponytail, pout, delusions of grandeur, etc... But come on, can any one of you look me seriously in the eye and tell me you've not felt the same about 'Sun' readers? Can any of you cross your heart and hope to die and tell me that you've never felt an uncontrollable urge to release the hounds on some woman with a double-barrelled surname and a son called Piers foisting a perfect end of year report on you? And can any one of you say in good conscience that you genuinely believe that the future of modern capitalism lies with the monkeys in suits of everybody's favourite business/reality show? Yeah, I didn't think so.

Examiner summary

This is very high quality work. It establishes and maintains an effective tone. The writer selects three 'victims' for Room 101 (about the right number) and talks about each one in a clever, interesting and witty way. He holds his audience by being provocative/controversial, overstating, asking questions, using rhetorical devices. It is well structured with an introduction to the objects of his satire, a lively discussion of each and then the pulling of it all together in a persuasive conclusion, making it difficult for the listener/reader to disagree. It is ambitiously and fluently written. It is sophisticated work with an impressively high level of accuracy. Grade A*(13/13 for content; 7/7 for sentence structure, punctuation and spelling).

Speeches/talks: how to go up the grades

- If writing a speech in class for Speaking and Listening, choose the topic carefully.
- In the exam you will be given a topic, but the subject will be one that is topical.
- Before starting to write, plan what you intend to say.
- Start by addressing your audience and keep that audience in mind throughout your speech.
- Choose information that will interest the audience and don't bombard them with facts and statistics – they will just switch off. Don't be afraid to draw on personal experience.
- Try to be ambitious in your writing and remember that mistakes cost you marks.

Putting it into practice

Discuss with a classmate what you have learnt in this section. Think about:

- the features of speeches and what makes them effective
- how speeches are made interesting for their audience.

My learning objectives ▼

- to practise using key features of writing a speech
- to develop a secure approach to writing a speech.

Exam practice and assessment

The speech below was written in response to the following question.

Write a speech intended for Year 6 pupils who will shortly be transferring to your school, telling them what to expect. (20 marks)

If you were attempting this task you would need to bear in mind some of the following.

▶ The audience, who are 11-year-olds. What will that mean as far as the way you write the piece is concerned?

▶ What the pupils will be feeling and what they will want to hear.

▶ How much you should cover.

▶ How they will feel once you have finished.

Hello Year 6,

Today I have come here to tell you a little bit about the school you will be going to in September, my school. I'll give you some information on what to expect and, hopefully, some useful advice!

First of all, it's important you listen to what the teachers tell you over your first few days and weeks: that information is valuable throughout your secondary school experience. For example, it is important you always bring the correct equipment to lessons. This is a small thing that you will be told when you start school, and will need to think about whenever you pack for a lesson.

Something you might have thoughts about is homework. You mightn't have received a very big amount of homework here, and feel worried about having to do it at the new school. I can assure you there is no need at all to feel worried. You won't get very much homework in the first week or so of school, and you'll find that the small amount is perfectly easy to cope with.

The workload will slowly increase, and by a few weeks in you will be getting two or three pieces of homework a night and thinking absolutely nothing of it! I promise you, it'll be really easy to handle, so don't fret about not being able to cope. You will.

Another thing I bet most of you are worried about is meeting new people. Starting a new school can be scary, believe me I know, and although you do have each other it is important to try and make friends. I started school not knowing anyone, because I was the only one going from my school. Although it was scary, I quickly made friends with a lot of people. This is because, and you should remember this, everyone is new. Some of those people who were brave enough to come up and say 'Hello' to me are now some of my best friends. So I really advise you to be the first to make an effort and be friendly. It really helps.

I'll just tell you a bit about your first day. It might seem intimidating having to be in a new school, not knowing where anything is or how to act, but you're not alone.

You'll each be assigned to a house, and the other Year 7s in that house will be your tutor group. Your tutor group will be the people you will have all your lessons with in Year 7, so you'll get to know them well. You'll also meet your tutor, who for the first two years of school will be the person you can go and talk to about anything, whether it's to ask about school work, or to discuss a problem you're having. Whatever it is, they are there to help you.

I think that's all you really need to know about starting in September, just don't panic and remember to be friendly!

I hope what I have told you is useful, and please feel free to ask me any questions.

Activity 1

If you were the examiner what mark would you give this speech? Use the mark scheme below to help you.

Activity 2

Now complete your own speech/talk.

Write a speech/talk on a subject of your own choice. This will be for people of your own age. (20 marks)

Peer/Self-assessment

1 Check your answer to Activity 2.
- Did you address your specified audience throughout?
- Is your speech well structured?
- Will your speech interest the audience?
- Is your speech accurately and effectively written?

2 Now try to grade your answer to Activity 2 using the mark scheme below.
You will need to be careful and precise in your marking.

Moving up the grades

Content and organisation (13 marks)

A (10–13 marks)
- sophisticated understanding of purpose of task
- sustained awareness of reader
- coverage is well judged, and detailed
- points are convincingly developed
- paragraphs are used to enhance effect
- sophisticated use of a range of stylistic devices
- appropriate and ambitious vocabulary.

C (7–9 marks)
- clear understanding of purpose of task
- clear awareness of audience
- good coverage
- ideas well shaped
- paragraphs used to structure writing
- style adapted to purpose/audience
- good range of vocabulary.

D (4–6 marks)
- shows awareness of purpose of task
- shows awareness of audience
- satisfactory coverage
- logical ordering of paragraphs
- attempts to adapt style to purpose/audience
- some range in vocabulary used.

Sentence structure, punctuation and spelling (7 marks)

A (6–7 marks)
- effective variation of sentence structures
- sophisticated use of a range of sentences to achieve effect
- punctuation is accurate and used confidently
- virtually all spelling is correct
- tenses are fully under control.

C (4–5 marks)
- a good range of sentences is used to achieve effects
- a range of punctuation is used accurately
- most spelling of familiar and less familiar words is accurate
- control of tense and agreement is secure.

D (2–3 marks)
- sentences are varied
- some control of a range of punctuation
- spelling of commonly used words is usually accurate
- control of tense and agreement is generally secure.

My learning objective ▼

- to learn about writing reviews, in particular of books, films and music.

Writing a review

Reviews are structured opinions of something read, seen or listened to.

Activity 1

Think about the last book you read, the last film you watched or the last CD you listened to. Explain what you thought of it, then read the notes below.

Reviews

We all have opinions and when it comes to films, books, music or television programmes we like to offer our views. The first thing we often say to a friend on leaving a cinema is 'Well, what did you think of that?' In replying we are reviewing what we have seen in an informal way. It is not a big jump from that to creating a written review.

Purpose	The purpose of a review is to give a reasoned opinion of a book, a film, a music CD, television programme, play, etc. We find reviews in newspapers and magazines; they vary in length, but you should be able to write one using one page of your exam answer book. Please remember it is not, in the case of a book or film, a retelling of what happens: this would ruin the reader's/filmgoer's enjoyment.
Format	There are some formatting issues to consider. You should start by using the title of the film/book/CD you are reviewing as a heading. In the case of a book, the name of the author should also appear, while a music CD review will indicate the name of the artist(s). The review should be written in paragraphs and will conclude with an overall opinion/recommendation. A star rating (one to five stars) may also be included.
Audience	In the exam the audience will be clearly stated – for example, 'for people of your own age'. What you write and how you write it will be dictated by this vital piece of information. The style of a review for a teenage magazine, obviously, will be quite different from one written for a national newspaper.

Main features of a review

▶ a heading, often the name of the book, film, television programme or CD

▶ an introductory paragraph which may give some background information, e.g. 'this is the third book in the … series.'

▶ middle paragraphs that discuss the book, CD, film etc. without giving too much away

▶ a concluding paragraph which is an opinion and perhaps a comparison of this with other work by the artist/writer. There will also be a recommendation and a star rating which seems to have become increasingly popular.

GradeStudio

Examiner tip

MAKE THE GRADE ✔

Choose some music, a film or book you know well. Think about format and what will go into your three to four paragraphs (introduction, outline, conclusion and opinion).

The reviews below will give you a good flavour of professionally written reviews. For each one, write down its features, then identify what they have in common.

THE TIMES

'The Other Half Lives' by Sophie Hannah

Ruth Bussey hasn't recovered from the guilt of a youthful transgression. When her boyfriend, Aidan Seed, suggests that they admit their deepest secrets she can imagine the love draining from his face. Aidan's secret is that he once killed a woman named Mary Trelease. Ruth is not only horrified by his crime but also knows Trelease who is very much alive. Frustrated 5 by Aidan's refusal to believe her, she approaches Charlotte Zailer, a police sergeant, who wonders 'Why would anyone confess to the murder of a woman who isn't dead?' Zailer is drawn into a web of lies that touches on her new relationship and her memories of a dead affair. Throughout the labyrinthine plot Hannah's characters retain our rapt attention.

THE INDEPENDENT

Whiteout (15)

100 mins. ★★
Starring: Kate Beckinsale, Gabriel Macht

Antarctica, six million square miles of ice and lonelier than death, is the setting
5 for this so-so thriller. Kate Beckinsale is a US marshal with implausibly perfect skin and a troubled past who finds a murder victim out on the plains of ice, so with a storm coming in and a killer on the loose she has her work cut out. Apart from a lascivious shot of his scantily clad star, director Dominic Sena keeps the action fairly swift under blizzard-like conditions: at times we seem to be
10 watching people fight inside a snow globe. And maybe my eyesight is also to blame: for most of the movie I thought the doctor actually played by Tom Skerritt was played by Kris Kristofferson.

It's taken David Gray four years to follow up 'Life in Slow Motion', and frankly, you have to wonder what's been holding him up, as these 11 pleasant, predictable songs represent no great development from the course of his previous work. The single 'Fugitive' opens proceedings in anthemic manner. From there it's business as usual, with twinkling 5 beds of arpeggiated guitar and rolling rhythms carrying Gray's world-weary drawl as he ponders his situation...

Musically the album is steadfastly stuck in the middle of the road, except for what sounds like the weird, sharp whine of cello pulled like a strand through 'First Chance'. Annie Lennox pops up to duet 10 on 'Full Steam Ahead', as does Jools Holland on 'Kathleen', neither shifting the results into a much more interesting position.

THE INDEPENDENT

David Gray – Draw the Line
★★

GradeStudio

Here are two book reviews written by students in response to the exam question below. Read the reviews and the examiner comments.

Write a review of a book you have read recently. (20 marks)

Student 1

The Empire of the Ants by Bernard Werber
Rating 10/10 Genre Sci-Fi/Factual
This is the best book I have ever read. The title may sound a little mundane but the story **defineately** is not. The setting is South of Paris in France where a man has just **inheritted** his uncle's house and discovers a book his uncle had **wrote**. There is a story running at the same time as this which is of an ants' nest waking up after winter. The story continues with the man reading more of his uncle's book on ants and the ants defending their nest. During both many interesting facts about the society of ants are put in. One of these is that ants war with each other and develop battlefield tactics. Another is that ants capture greenfly and take them back to their nest; there they feed the greenfly and harvest their honeydew for eating, much like dairy farmers.
In the end, the man is led down into the cellar where he'd been warned never to go because his dog went down there. He has to get through many obstacles and rats until he reaches an underground laboratory. On the ant side of the story the main ant character becomes a queen of a new nest and the old one she came from is burnt down by some orphans, making her resentful of humans. The laboratory the man entered turned out to be...
I'd better not write any so as not to spoil the ending.

Examiner comment

The student has a basic idea of how to set about a review. For example, he is conscious that he may give too much away. There is an attempt at a format and the review is mostly accurately written, however, the work could be better organised/paragraphed. He becomes a little too involved in the nuts and bolts of the story and could stand back a bit more. A more convincing case could be made for the book, after all it is the best book he has read. Some of the more mundane bits of information could have been left out. Some glaring errors need to be corrected (highlighted in the first five lines).

Addressing the above points would get this work into C grade and beyond. As it stands, the review would be awarded a D grade (6/13 for content and organisation; 3/7 for sentence structure, punctuation and spelling).

Student 2

Black or White, Rich or Poor, Powerful or Prejudiced ... Nought or Cross?

This book is not a fantasy, there are no dragons, witches or time machines, in fact, the setting is in many ways identical to that of the modern day; however in other ways, it could not be more different. Malorie Blackman's latest thriller, Noughts and Crosses, explores the taboo issue of racialism, in a totally reversed view of society, where the black man is the predator, the ruler, and the white man is the inferior prey. In a world where there is no grey, where Christmas is Crossmas, all terrorists are white, and the name of Mohammed rules the House of Commons the scene is perfect for a tale of violence, hatred and thwarted love between nought and cross.

What is the book about?

Noughts and Crosses is a book about the struggles that one nought boy, Callum, and another cross girl, Stephy, face. Although best friends, Callum leads a life in his father's footsteps, of terrorism, bombs and violence, whereas Stephy has a more privileged and important life-style, attending private school and living as the daughter of the cross priminister. Opposites attract, and Callum and Stephy struggle as they begin to face some of the toughest decisions and most heart-breaking decisions in life.

Why did I enjoy this book?

Malorie Blackman writes with flair to create a world perfect for escapist reading, different in many ways from the modern day. The story contains something for everyone's taste, violence, hatred, and then at the other end of the scale, love and a wish for peace and harmony. I enjoyed this book as the characters were very easy to relate to, and the story was unpredictable with many twists and turns, the ending particularly moved me, and could bring even the harshest of critics to tears.

I would recommend this book to a teenager who enjoys a tale of unpredictability and like me, likes to ponder over the morals of the story, and be moved by its effect on how you see your life for weeks after reading it. This book makes a real impression

Examiner comment

Content/Organisation

The first thing we notice is that there is no heading, i.e. the name of the book, the author and publisher. This is not an oversight. The student has done this deliberately to shape her review in her own way. Examiners always allow for individual approaches provided they are effective.

The first paragraph draws the reader in skilfully and only then are the title and author named. Normally sub-headings are not used in reviews. They are used here but are not really necessary. Enough of the story is given to suggest the flavour of the book, but too much is not given away. The opinion/recommendation is well handled and persuades the reader that this book is well worth reading.

Technical accuracy

She is obviously a fluent writer with a good vocabulary. There is an ability to shape and vary (sentence type and length) the writing to interest the reader. However there are punctuation and spelling errors – for example, no inverted commas around the name of the book, the misspelling 'priminister', the use of a comma instead of a colon in the third line of the last section, the use of a comma rather than a full stop after 'turns' in the penultimate paragraph and the omission of a full stop right at the end.

This means that the content mark would be high but the accuracy mark good but not as good as it might have been. Overall this work was awarded a secure A grade (11/13 for content and organisation; 6/7 for sentence structure, punctuation and spelling).

Moving up the grades

Do not retell what happens in the piece you are reviewing as this would spoil the enjoyment for the reader. Remember to think about the structure of your review and the audience you are writing for.

Putting it into practice

Discuss with a classmate what you have learnt in this section. Think about:

- the features of reviews and what makes them effective
- how reviews are structured opinions of something read, seen or listened to.

My learning objectives ▼
- to practise using key features of reviews
- to develop a secure approach to writing a review.

Exam practice and assessment

A review is often written of a live performance.
Read the example below, written by a student for the exam.

'Seusical the Musical' is a theatre production based on the novels of Dr Seuss. All of his stories have been combined to create one big production by the drama students at the Lamproom Theatre.

'Seusical' follows the adventures of Horton, an elephant who one day hears mysterios voices coming from a speck of dust. He discovers that within the tiny speck of dust exists the tiniest planet in the universe which is called Whoville. In this little planet lives a race of creatures called Who's who are in danger and so it is left to Horton to be their protector. However, Horton is ridiculed by the animals in the Jungle of Nool because he persists in his beliefs of the Whos. The only animal who does'nt mock Horton is Gertrude McFuze who admires and falls in love with him.

Meanwhile the cat in the hat plays the narrator and the devils advocate throughout the show. Many of the actors took my breath away as you could tell they through themselves into their characters.

One of the characters who was impressive was the mischevous cat who kept coming into the action with great enthusiasm on several occasions causing conflict between the other characters.

Also another character caught my attention which was the 'Sour Kangaroo', her voice was so powerful it had me strapped to my seat.

Beautiful coloured costumes also attracted my attention as they were blindingly bright almost taking the spotlight from the whole performance.

However throughout the show I noticed at one point when all of the characters entered the stage they did'nt know where to stand and it was really cramped as there was little space available for all of them to fit.

It was a brilliant idea to use audience participation at the begining of the show, they asked the audience questions and at the end they ran into the crowd.

Overall, I recommend that families should go and see this entertaining and enthusiastic performance as it will easily entertain the children.

I give this theatre production a **** rating.

Activity 3

Compare this review with the others in this section. What grade would you award it? Refer to the grade descriptions.
- Does this sound like a review?
- What features of a review have you noticed?
- Does the introduction do its job?
- Are the central paragraphs well organised? Can you suggest any improvements?
- Is the review effectively concluded?
- How accurate is the writing? Proofread the review and correct any errors.

Activity 4

Now complete your own review.

Write a review of a book, film or music CD that you have recently read, seen or listened to. (20 marks)

GradeStudio

Examiner tip

When writing a review choose something you are familiar with and give your views in an interesting and honest way.

Peer/Self-assessment

1 Check your answers to Activity 4.
   - Did you choose your subject carefully?
   - Did you provide a title?
   - Did you introduce the reader to the subject of your review?
   - In giving information about the book/film/CD were you selective, remembering not to give too much away?
   - Did you provide a conclusion?
   - Did you give a clear reaction?
   - Did you take care to ensure a high level of accuracy in your writing?

2 Now try to grade your answer to Activity 4 using the mark scheme below. You will need to be careful and precise in your marking.

Moving up the grades

Content and organisation (13 marks)

A (10–13 marks)
   - sophisticated understanding of purpose of task
   - sustained awareness of reader
   - coverage is well judged, and detailed
   - points are convincingly developed
   - paragraphs are used to enhance effect
   - sophisticated use of a range of stylistic devices
   - appropriate and ambitious vocabulary.

C (7–9 marks)
   - clear understanding of purpose of task
   - clear awareness of audience
   - good coverage
   - ideas well shaped
   - paragraphs used to structure writing
   - style adapted to purpose/audience
   - a good range of vocabulary.

D (4–6 marks)
   - shows awareness of purpose of task
   - shows awareness of audience
   - satisfactory coverage
   - logical ordering of paragraphs
   - attempts to adapt style to purpose/audience
   - some range in vocabulary used.

Sentence structure, punctuation and spelling (7 marks)

A (6–7 marks)
   - effective variation of sentence structures
   - sophisticated use of a range of sentences to achieve effect
   - punctuation is accurate and used confidently
   - virtually all spelling is correct
   - tenses are fully under control.

C (4–5 marks)
   - a good range of sentences is used to achieve effects
   - a range of punctuation is used accurately
   - most spelling of familiar and less familiar words is accurate
   - control of tense and agreement is secure.

D (2–3 marks)
   - sentences are varied
   - some control of a range of punctuation
   - spelling of commonly used words is usually accurate
   - control of tense and agreement is generally secure.

3 Controlled assessment guide

What is controlled assessment?

Your GCSE exam is made up of two parts:

▶ external assessment – the exam for Paper 1 and Paper 2
▶ controlled assessment – where your teacher will give you details of your tasks for Unit 3 and Unit 4.

For all of your written controlled assessment, you will be given the questions in advance and your teacher will provide guidance. You will have an opportunity to study for them. Your teacher will tell you how much time you have to prepare for each one.

When you write your final version, you will be in 'controlled conditions'. This means there will be a time limitation, and you will not be allowed to discuss your work with other students or your teacher. In your Reading assigments you will be allowed to have clean copies of the text you are writing about, plus one A4 sheet of notes to help you. These notes must not contain a draft essay or an essay plan. In the Writing assignments you will not be allowed access to dictionaries or thesauri. You can complete your work on a word processor but you must not have access to spell checker or grammar programmes. At this stage, your teacher will not be able to help you. Once you have finished your work you will not be able to change it, so you must take great care to do your best.

What is it worth?

Your controlled assessment is worth 60% of your marks, so it is important that you do well if you want to get a good grade.

Unit 3: Literary texts and open writing

What is it worth? Unit 3 is worth 40% of your marks, 20% for reading and 20% for writing.

What is assessed in reading?

You will need to write:

- an essay which makes links between a Shakespeare play and a poem drawn from a range chosen from the WJEC Poem Collection. This is worth 10% of your marks and you will have 4 hours to complete this work
- an essay on a Different Cultures prose text. This is worth 10% of your marks and you will have 2 hours to complete this work.

What is assessed in writing?

You will need to write:

- one piece of first-person writing
- one piece of third-person writing.

You will have two hours to complete both pieces of work.

General titles will be given to you for these tasks.

Unit 4: Speaking and Listening

What is it worth? Unit 4 is worth 20% of your marks.

What is assessed?

Your Speaking and Listening skills will be tested in three ways. You will have to:

- give an individual presentation to a group
- take part in group discussion
- show your skill in role-play.

The tasks will cover the following areas:

- communicating and adapting language
- interacting and responding
- creating and sustaining roles.

What does controlled assessment for GCSE English Language look like?

Unit 3: Literary reading and creative writing

What is it worth? Unit 3 is worth 30% of your marks, 15% for reading and 15% for writing.

What is assessed in reading?

The reading part of your assessment is known as 'Studying written language'. You will need to write an essay on a play or a novel. This is worth 15% of your marks. You will be given 2 hours to complete this task.

What is assessed in writing?

The writing part of your assessment is known as 'Using language'. You will need to write:

- one piece of descriptive writing which is worth 7.5% of your marks
- one piece of narrative/expressive writing which is worth 7.5% of your marks.

You will have 2 hours to complete these two pieces.

General titles will be given to you for these tasks.

Unit 4: Using Language (Speaking and Listening) and Studying Spoken Language

What is it worth? Unit 4 is worth 30% of your marks: 20% for Speaking and Listening and 10% for Studying Spoken Language.

What is assessed in Speaking and Listening?

Your Speaking and Listening skills will be tested in three ways. It is worth 20% of your marks. You will have to:

- give an individual presentation to a group
- take part in group discussion
- show your skill in role-play.

The tasks will cover the following areas:

- communicating and adapting language
- interacting and responding
- creating and sustaining roles.

What is assessed in Studying Spoken Language?

You will need to produce an essay on an aspect of spoken language (variations, choices or change in spoken language). This work could be on your own or others' use of spoken language and is worth 10% of the total mark.

If you are taking English Language, support for Studying Spoken Language can be found on pages 148–169 of this book.

4 Studying spoken language

What is involved in studying spoken language?

If you are taking GCSE English Language, you will study change, choice or variation in spoken language. This work could be about your own or someone else's use of spoken language, and you could study it as a recording, a transcript or a recollection.

How will my work be assessed?

Your work will be assessed through writing an essay in controlled conditions. It is worth 10% of your marks. You will be assessed against Assessment Objective 2:

▶ Understand variations in spoken language, explaining why language changes in relationship to contexts.

▶ Assess the impact of spoken language choices in their own and others' use.

Remember that the examiner will be looking to see:

▶ how well you understand the way language varies

▶ how you relate language to the situation in which it occurs

▶ how you understand the impact of language choices in your own and in other people's use of language.

What do spoken language study activities look like?

Opposite are some examples of the general types of activities. These will help you understand what you are preparing for as you work through this section. Your teachers will outline the details of your own specific activity.

How spoken language is used in different contexts

This activity is about language change – the way we change our language depending on context (where we are, who we are with). You will be assessed on your understanding of how a situation affects the vocabulary and voice of the speakers. You will reflect on and explain your own and others' uses of language in some of the following situations:

- in the workplace
- in the classroom
- on television
- in problem-solving (giving directions, explaining a procedure, making decisions).

> This question is about language context – the way we choose our language depending on where we are.

> You will be assessed on your understanding of how a situation affects the vocabulary and voice of the speakers.

How spoken language is adapted to different listeners

This activity is about language choice – the way we choose to speak depending on who the listener is. You will be assessed on your understanding of how words and voice are chosen and shaped for different listeners. You will explore how your own and others' use of language is adapted in the contexts of wider language use and variation. The following situations would provide appropriate contexts:

- responding to older or younger listeners
- talking to peers and family
- responding to people in authority
- responding to strangers.

> This question is about language choice – the way we change how we speak depending on who the listener is.

> You will be assessed on your understanding of how you shape and choose your words and voice to suit the needs of your listener.

The effects of choices in the use of standard and non-standard forms of spoken language

This activity is about language variation – the way we vary our use of standard and non-standard forms of language, and reflect regional or specialist language. You will be assessed on how you recognise the choice of standard and non-standard speech and appreciate their effects. You will need to demonstrate your understanding of the reasons for and effects of these choices, and how they may vary over time and place.

The following situations would provide appropriate contexts:

- using non-standard forms to peers and family
- using standard forms to strangers and those in authority
- the effects of standard and non-standard forms in television and radio advertising.

> This question is about language variation – the way we use language correctly, informally, and reflect regional or specialist language

> You will be assessed on how you recognise standard and non-standard speech and appreciate their effects.

What will I need to do?

Research and planning

This is where you gather your information and spoken language samples in preparation for your individual responses for assessment.

- You will have around 8 hours.
- Your teacher can give you general guidance and advice.
- Make sure you understand what the activity requires and how to prepare.
- You can research, make recordings and transcribe your samples, or discuss and write down your examples of language use.
- You will need to make notes and could keep a log or notebook.

Work with features of spoken language
(see 'Language change, choice and variation' page 158)

You will need to understand the features of spoken language that relate to your activity. Spoken language varies enormously depending on where we are, who we are and why we are speaking. For example:

- **change** – how does our language change to fit different contexts (for example in the playground or in a doctor's surgery)?
- **choice** – how do we choose our language to suit specific listeners (for example with children or with older people)?
- **variation** – how do we vary our use of standard and non-standard language and reflect regional or specialist language (for example we might speak in dialect, or use slang with friends and formal language with a teacher)?

Work with recordings, transcripts and recollections
(see 'Capturing spoken language', page 152)

You may:
- record yourself or your friends and family using simple recording devices in a clear, useful and reasonable way
- turn your recordings or recollections into usable and helpful information by creating transcripts
- learn how to transcribe spoken language in a helpful way
- analyse and use this information in your essay.

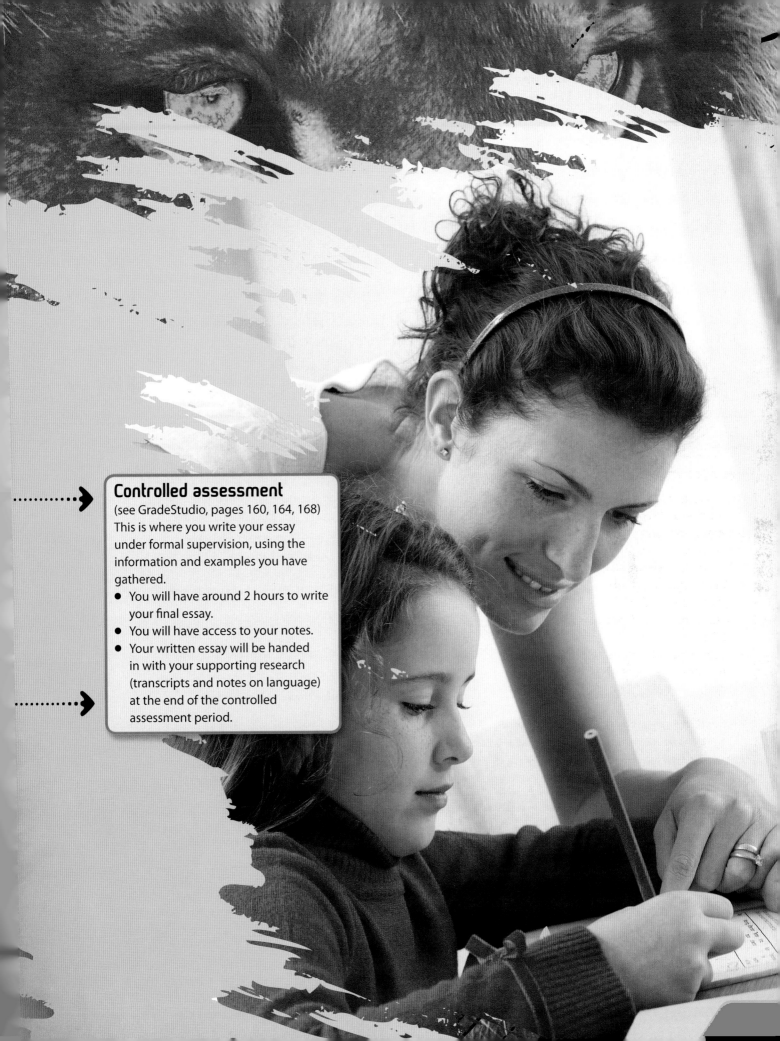

Controlled assessment

(see GradeStudio, pages 160, 164, 168)
This is where you write your essay
under formal supervision, using the
information and examples you have
gathered.

- You will have around 2 hours to write
  your final essay.
- You will have access to your notes.
- Your written essay will be handed
  in with your supporting research
  (transcripts and notes on language)
  at the end of the controlled
  assessment period.

Making a recording

Recording language digitally

You may need to make a record of spoken language to help you understand and explain key features. It is often best to make a recording with a mobile phone, cassette recorder or other digital recording device. This means that:

▷ You will have a permanent record that you can replay many times.

▷ You will have an accurate recording of speech.

▷ You will be able to hear not just what people say but how they say it.

▷ You can record from real life, television or radio. Sports commentaries, chat shows, radio phone-ins and quiz shows all work well.

Activity 1

1   Try out your own recording of language. A trial run now can save you time later. You could make a recording that helps with your own controlled assessment task, or carry out the activity below.

> Record a small group of boys and a small group of girls, to see if males and females talk differently.
> You could ask them to discuss the questions below and make notes from the recording.
> Compare your findings with other people's results.
> - Are females or males more polite?
> - Do females or males most try to show off (telling jokes, dominating)?
> - Do males or females try to include everyone in the conversation?
> - What do boys talk about?
> - What do girls talk about?

2   To ensure your recording is as useful as possible, use a checklist like the one below and update it with your own experience.

Making a good recording	Capturing the sample you need
• make sure you have the permission of the people you are recording • make sure you have enough recording space on your device • don't have too big a group – too many voices can be confusing • keep the recording device near the people speaking • if people are uncomfortable at first because you are recording, you could start when they have relaxed • make the recording in a quiet place, if that is possible.	• brief the group with a definite topic to discuss, so you get the outcomes you need, related to your task • take your recording somewhere quiet and replay it • choose the section that is most interesting and useful for the controlled assessment activity you have chosen.

3   Once you have tried your recording, note down how well it went. Is there anything you might improve next time? For example:

What worked?	Did anything go wrong?	What might work next time?
There was a lot of discussion	Too many people talking at once	Try it with a smaller group
The recording was clear enough		

Once you have a good recording you can use it to make a transcript to analyse and comment on. You have a record to check how people spoke as well as what they said.

Recording language using notes

You could also record your language using notes, which can be efficient if you are listening for a specific language feature. You could record it more easily using a well-planned table. To work well it must:

▷ be easy to use

▷ record information about speakers

▷ record something about the context.

Activity 2

Try making notes of spoken language. You could make notes to help with your own controlled assessment task, or use the topic from Activity 1 and choose specific language features. You could complete a table like the one below and comment on what you think the results mean.

Group gender m/f	Group names used	No. of swearing incidents (taboo language)	Situation or context	Subject discussed
M	Boys, mun, guys, lads	/ / / / / / / / / / / / / / / = 15	Outside form room	Football teams, money
F	Babes, guys, girls, mun	/ / / / / / / / / / / / / / / / = 16	Lunch room queue	Food, films
M & F				

My learning objectives ▼
- to understand some key features of a transcript
- to make a transcript.

Using transcripts

A transcript is spoken language written down, so it is easier to analyse the features and make comments.

Activity 1

Speech is usually written as a transcript, as this shows the features of speech better than standard writing. Punctuation is replaced by pauses and underlining to show emphasis. Compare the two ways of writing the same speech below. What do you learn from the transcript that you don't get from the standard written version?

Pause of 2 seconds as customer decides.

Extra stress on type of drink shown by underlined word.

Other effects such as coughs or smiles are shown in brackets.

Written language

C: A can of coke please.
S: Diet coke or regular coke?
C: Regular please.
S: That's sixty-five pence.
C: No, I want two cans.
S: That's one pound thirty then.

Spoken language

C: Er (2) can of coke please
S: Diet or regular?
C: (2) <u>Regular</u> please
S: Sixty five p then please (coughs)
C: No, I want <u>two</u> cans
S: (tut) (.) that'll be one thirty then

Customer overlaps and interrupts the shopkeeper.

Extra stress on number of cans.

Activity 2

Now look at the statement below.

No, I'm not going to London tomorrow.

When this statement is spoken, the use of pauses and emphasis on different words can change its meaning. Read these two transcripts and see how pause, emphasis and facial expression can change its meaning.

1 No (.) I'm not going to London <u>tomorrow</u> (*I'm going the day after*)

2 (Smiles) No <u>I'm</u> not going to London tomorrow (*someone else is going, I got out of it*)

Write a transcript of the same words to show the meaning *I'm not going to London I'm going somewhere else.*

Key transcript symbols

Symbol	What the symbol means	What the symbol tells us
(.)	A pause less than half a second long	How speech is punctuated and it shows thinking time Oh (.) right (.) ok then (.)
(2)	A longer timed pause of two seconds	Thinking is going on or perhaps the speaker is waiting for a reply
Underlined word(s)	Extra emphasis on these words	Which words are important
Can you get the phone? 　　　Sorry really busy.	Overlaps – a vertical line shows the words said at the same time	This can be rude – when it's an interruption, or just a result of talking (or wanting to answer) very quickly
(coughs)	Other noises	Other contextual details
T, S	Initial of speaker	In the example on this page, T for teacher, S for student

Activity 3

1 This transcript was made from a recording of the start of a lesson. The student was looking at how teachers and students use spoken language in the classroom (context).

Read the transcript and check what the transcript symbols mean using the table above.

2 Now make your own transcript.

- If you have a choice of recordings, start with the one with fewest voices.
- If it is your first transcript, select no more than 30 seconds.
- Transcribing takes time and patience. Use headphones or ear pieces if you have them. Work on only 5 seconds of recording at a time, less if you need to. Listen carefully and replay the recording as often as you need to get an accurate transcript.
- Make your transcript, using the relevant transcript symbols.
- Think carefully about or discuss with your teacher the kinds of spoken language features that you will be looking out for.
- Use a highlighter to pick out features such as questions, commands, politeness, topic-setting, hesitation, and overlapping speech. Think about and discuss with your teacher why these features are important.

> This opening section explains the setting and speakers.

> Overlapping speech

The class takes place in a secondary school, first lesson of the day on a Tuesday. It is a history lesson for Year 11 pupils both male and female. T =Teacher, S1, S2, S3 = students in the class.

T: right everyone, settle down (.) settle down (.) are we all here then? (.) ok
5 (.) Ravi, where were you on Monday? (.) not like you to be off (.) nothing to do with the homework was it?
S1: 　　　no sir
T: (.) ok then (.) let's see what you've remembered (.) why do most historians say we should study the D-Day landings?
10 S2: sir, erm (.) because it was the biggest sea-borne invasion ever?
T: yes, good Susan (.) and what reasons do other historians give?
S3: was it cos Roosevelt wanted to get Europe back before winter sir?
T: hmm (.) you're all very sharp today, we must have had three shredded wheat (.) ok (.) what was the code name for the landings (.) Jane?
15 S3: Overlord sir
T: very good Jane (.) and the code names of the beaches where the US Army landed? You might remember it from the film Saving Private Ryan
S2: Utah?
T: excellent (.) yes Utah and Omaha beach as well

My learning objectives ▼

- to understand how to work with spoken language recollection
- to bring together a spoken language recollection.

Using spoken language recollection

Spoken language recollection is where you use your knowledge and memory of speech patterns and habits used by many different people in many different situations.

For good spoken language recollection, you need a range of words, information and language. Try to ask a variety of different people: old, young, male, female, local people and people in other parts of the United Kingdom.

Activity 1

1 To work with language recollection in a way that helps with your own controlled assessment task, use the activities below.

- Find out what different words/phrases people use to describe how they feel when they are really pleased or really fed up.
- Find out the different words people use to describe a specific item. Choose items that most interest you, or you could try some of the following: friend, bread roll, mid-morning snack, a foolish person, bad tempered, attractive.

2 To build up your use of language recollection:
- talk with your friends and family; notice the phrases they use and make a note of them as quickly as possible afterwards
- discuss words in a group; share and note down words and phrases (working in a group can help you record more information)
- use the Internet, especially if you belong to a social networking site and know people who might use different words/phrases across the country.

Activity 2

Create a table like the one below so that you can log the variations of words and phrases.

Standard English	Grandparent/ older person	Parent /guardian	Friends	Local word	My words
pleased	glad, happy, thrilled	beaming, landed	chuffed, well happy, stoked, made up	landed	
to truant	mitch, bunk off	bunk off, truant	do a bunk, hookey, skip	mitch	
friend					

- Listen out for words to add to your list; you will find you hear them often.
- You may want to add extra information about how some of the words have been used, e.g. what was being described.
- Keep a notebook so you can add words over time.

When you explore words/phrases, watch out for the way language varies. You might find examples of the things listed below. It might be useful to add observations like this to your notes about language recollection: you could add them to your table.

▷ **language affected by location:** the way people speak often reflects where they live. This can result in:

   ▷ different accents (the sound of words), for example Cockney, West Country, Geordie

   ▷ different dialects (words that can be specific to a region), for example the Lancashire words *nesh* (weak) and *mardy* (complaining).

▷ **new meanings for old words:** *mouse* has a new meaning now, so do *chip*, Mac, *wireless* and *mega*. (A wireless is what people called a radio about 50 years ago.)

▷ **new words for new inventions:** we now have a *Nokia*, a *Dyson*, an *iPod*, *downloads*, *uploads* and *Facebook*.

▷ **language created for fun:** for example, young people create and use slang words such as *wicked, sick, mint* just as the generations before them had *bad, groovy* and *hip*

▷ **cross-over words:** for example, dialect words that are only used by older people. For example, in south Wales *tidy* is a dialect word with a wide range of meanings. A long distance is *a tidy step*, a nice young person is *a tidy boy or girl*, *to talk tidy* is to talk sensibly, and if you mean *oh good* you just say *tidy*. Young people tend not to use it.

Your table may be a useful source of spoken language recollection for your controlled assessment task.

GradeStudio

Examiner tips

● When asking about words/phrases, people may just use the ones you mention. For example, if you ask for the word they used for playing truant, they may say 'playing truant'. Instead you could try asking, 'What did you used to call it when you or someone else took a day off school without permission?'

● Older people and parents may want to give you only Standard English words, so emphasise that you want local words and informal words.

● Ask people to recollect as many words as they can – don't just ask for one.

Language change

My learning objectives ▼

- to understand how spoken language changes in different contexts
- to analyse a transcript and explain how language changes.

Language change is how we change our language depending on the context we are in (for example in the playground or in a doctor's surgery). To explain how language changes in context, it is useful to explore situations that strongly affect the way language is used. For example, we don't speak the same way on the television as we do in the classroom; we don't speak the same way in the playground as we do in the doctor's surgery.

Below is a brief example of the kind of approach you might take, using the following sample activity.

Explain how teachers and students use spoken language in the classroom.

Activity 1

In this sample we are working with the transcript from Activity 3 on page 155. Read the transcript and answer the questions opposite.

> The class takes place in a secondary school, first lesson of the day on a Tuesday. It is a history lesson for Year II pupils both male and female. T =Teacher, SI, S2, S3 = students in the class.
>
> T: <u>right everyone, settle down</u> (.) settle down (.) are we all here then? (.) ok
> 5 (I) Ravi, where were you on Monday? (.) not like you to be off (.) nothing to do with the homework was it?
> SI: | no sir ·· Overlapping speech
> T: (.) ok then (.) let's see what you've remembered (I) why do <u>most</u> historians say we should study the D-Day landings?
> 10 S2: sir, erm (.) because it was the biggest sea-borne invasion ever?
> T: <u>yes</u>, good Susan (I) and what reasons do other historians give?
> S3. was it cos Roosevelt wanted to get Europe back before winter sir?
> T: hmm (I) you're all very sharp today, we must have had three shredded wheat (I) ok (.) what was the code name for the landings (.) Jane?
> 15 S3: Overlord sir
> T: <u>very</u> good Jane (.) and the code names of the beaches where the US Army landed? You might remember it from the film Saving Private Ryan
> S2: Utah?
> T: <u>excellent</u> (.) yes Utah and Omaha beach as well

Use these questions to explore the transcript opposite. The questions in bold can help you explore language change in any context.

1 **What effect does the situation or context have here?** Classrooms have unwritten rules that everyone follows. Can you suggest some?

2 **Who sets the topic?** How does the teacher signal that the lesson is about to start, and get it going in the right direction?

3 **Which words used here are specific to the subject?** Specialist language is always a feature of language change, for example historical terms such as *historians*, *sea-borne invasion* and *Roosevelt*.

4 **Who uses questions?** Who uses the most questions in the transcript opposite? Why? Can you find examples of open and closed questions in the transcript opposite?
   - An **open question** is one that can have several different answers and they may be used to generate opinions and start discussion. For example: *Why do most historians say we should study the D-Day landings?*
   - A **closed question** is one that has a short, definite answer, sometimes just yes or no. Closed questions are used to check facts, for example: *What was the code-name for the landings, Jane?*
   - **Questions used to control** *Are we all here, then?*

5 **Who uses commands and how are they used?**
   - Teachers usually make their commands and their ways of saying 'wrong' polite, e.g. *not quite*. Why do you think that is?
   - Find one polite statement in the transcript opposite that is really an instruction or command.

6 **Pauses are important – what do they say?** Find examples of pauses used by the teacher. Why do you think they have been used?

7 **How do the speakers connect with each other?** Why do you think the teacher uses the word 'we', e.g. *We must have had three shredded wheat?* Why does he say, *You might remember it from the film 'Saving Private Ryan'?*

8 **Who praises?** In a classroom context it is usually the teacher who gives praise. Find two examples of praise in the transcript. Why is praise important? Why does the teacher praise the whole class as well as individuals?

GradeStudio

Here are extracts from two student responses to the sample question below about language change, using the transcript on page 158. Read the answers together with the examiners comments, then check what you have learnt and try putting it into practice.

Explain how teachers and students use spoken language in the classroom. (20 marks)

Now, compare the differences between a C grade answer and an A grade answer.

C grade answer

Student 1

From the opening of the essay

In the classroom the teacher wants to be in control so that everybody learns. He or she also needs to join up the learning so that one lesson follows on from the one before it. The students probably want an easy lesson. The teacher makes sure that the class gets ready to learn and quickly checks attendance for the register. We can see it is a man teacher as the students call him 'sir'. He starts with a general question that anyone can try to answer.

> Some reasonable ideas here about the situation, but needs examples.

> Quite a good opening. Some useful points on purpose.

From the middle paragraphs of the essay

The teacher reminds the students of where they'd got to last lesson and does a quick check on what they remember, 'What was the code name for the landings, Jane?' The teacher gets more friendlier once he starts to get correct answers, 'very good Jane'. This praise is important as students like to feel that they are getting it right. But some students might feel left out as he only asks Jane. He should give more of them a chance to answer.

> Some better understanding here and evidence in support, but the student misses the importance pause (.) between the question and the choice of who should answer.

From the ending of the essay

Overall the teacher chooses language to create a good mood and adapts his language so that the students can understand him. The teacher talks the most because he knows the most. He mentions a well-known film to try and connect with his students. My teacher does this but he always chooses a film we've never heard of.

> Some sensible summing up but short on examples. The reason given for the teacher talking the most is not the best one. The last sentence is not relevant.

Examiner comment

The extracts from the answer show several good and valid points and it is coherent. However, the answer also needs to go into more detail and provide examples. Some ideas are too simple, like the 'easy lesson' (in fact, the students seem keen to learn). The middle section is better, with more examples and a comment about the mood 'The teacher gets (more) friendlier' – but the grammar is weak here. The answer begins to explain the effects of speech change and begins to analyse how speech is used in the classroom. The ending misses opportunities to add supporting evidence and could develop the idea about 'Saving Private Ryan'. It is a reasonable answer in its way, but misses some opportunities. Grade C.

MAKE THE GRADE
MAKE THE GRADE

Student 2

From the opening of the essay

The male teacher starts to get the class ready to learn by using the command 'settle down'. He is like a conductor controlling an orchestra. First he wants quiet. He asks the class a general open question and emphasises the word 'most' so that the students know there is more than one answer. He says 'OK then' which is another way of saying let's get started. Susan answers correctly and the teacher praises her, but he wants to push them further so he asks for the other reasons.

> A strong start picking up some subtle ideas about the context.

From the middle paragraphs of the essay

The teacher must be quite happy with the class because he praises them and makes a joke about shredded wheat. He uses the word 'we' a lot which gives the good feeling that they are all working together. He asks Jane a closed question which she answers correctly. His praise of Jane adds, I think, to the positive mood in the class.

> Very good attention to detail here.

From the ending of the essay

Overall the teacher chooses language to create a positive mood 'very good', 'excellent' and adapts his language so that the students feel included. He mentions a well-known film, 'Saving Private Ryan', to try and make the D-Day battles seem more relevant to his young students. He ends this sequence with his highest praise for the speaker, 'Excellent', and finishes by completing the answer more thoroughly.

Examiner comment

This answer is thorough, more detailed and shows sound understanding. It pays attention to the choice of language, the use of questions and commands, the pauses and the teacher's use of emphasis. It is nicely tentative in its conclusions 'it seems', 'he may', where the previous answer was a little dogmatic. The answer is sensitive to mood, and how it is created, and uses examples to support the main points. The candidate is able to recognise open and closed, and general and more focused questions. A strong grade A.

MOVING UP THE GRADES

Language change: how to go up the grades

To move up the grades you need to be sensitive to the tone, so not just what is being said but **how** it is being said. This means looking carefully at the context or situation and thinking about how it may be affecting the language. The idea in the C grade answer is undeveloped. It makes assumptions, such as 'The students probably want an easy lesson', which have no support in the text. The Grade A answer is thorough and detailed using examples to support the main points. The ideas show clear understanding and the answer is able to demonstrate this with the use of evidence.

Putting it into practice

You have learnt that language changes to suit different situations and roles; you have explored language change in a classroom context and also the qualities of a C grade answer and an A grade answer.

Use what you have learnt when you look at language change in any context, and use these **key questions** to help you:

- What kind of language is expected here?
- What kind of behaviour is expected here?
- Who is likely to control the topic and decide who can participate?
- Is there a special vocabulary the speakers use?

When writing your essay, remember to:

- quote examples from the transcript to support your ideas
- be tentative when writing conclusions, e.g. 'this **could** be because he lacks confidence'
- start by writing about the language and behaviour expected in your chosen situation
- look out for features such as politeness, questions, commands and praise or blame and what these might mean.

- to understand how we choose language for different listeners
- to analyse a transcript and show the significance of language choice.

Language choice

GradeStudio

Examiner tip

MAKE THE GRADE ✓ MAKE THE GRADE

Always ask these key questions of language choice.
- What kind of language choices are made by the participants here?
- Who adapts most to their listeners' expectations?
- Does anyone seem to speak down or raise their speech level?
- Who seems most comfortable in the discussion? Who seems most awkward?

Language choice is how we choose our language depending on who the listener is (for example with children or older people). To show the significance of language choice it is useful to explore situations that strongly affect the way language fits the listener. For example, we don't speak the same way to older or younger people as we do to our friends. We don't speak to strangers or those in authority in the way we speak to our family.

Below is a brief example of the kind of approach you might take, using the following sample exam question.

Show that you understand the significance of the language choices made by people with and without authority.

In this sample we are working with a transcript made from a recording. Read the transcript, then answer the questions opposite.

The transcript is of an interview between a parent and a headteacher. The parent has brought her son with her; he seems uninterested in the discussion. The headteacher has the administrator with her. It is lunchtime.

Headteacher: (quietly to the administrator) I can tell this parent's going to be a pain (.) try and get some really good facts (.) throw her off ok (3)

Administrator: ok

HT: (very quietly) waste of time. (3) (louder) Miss Lovering (.) hello

5 **Parent:** (to son) sit down (1) I am here today because I am appalled at the standard of food served in your school

HT: well I don't serve any food in this school which is why I've brought my colleague along Alex Bradley-Hooters

Parent: well maybe he can explain then

10 **Administrator:** our food is of high quality from (.) trusted and (.) inspected farmers around the country the food (.) the food is pre-prepared and brought in

Parent: huh

Administrator: in vacuum packs to ensure freshness (1)

HT: there you have it it's absolutely perfect food there's not a problem

From a role-play on the inter-group GCSE English Speaking and Listening DVD, 2007

Activity 1

Use the questions below to explore the transcript. The questions in bold are useful to explore language choice in any context.

1   **What effects do the language choices of the speakers have?**
    The language styles of the headteacher are quite different a) when she is talking quietly to the administrator and b) when she is addressing the parent. Pick out two examples of a) non-standard and b) standard language.

2   **Which of the listeners doesn't have to change their style?**
    Who is adapting their style more, the teacher, the parent or the administrator? Who seems most at ease with the style?

3   **How is the seriousness of the topic signalled by the speakers?** How formal is the parent's language choice here? Choose one or two phrases as examples.

4   **Who uses confident and fluent language?** Often, confident people speak fluently and nervous or unsure people speak hesitantly.
    ● Nervous or unsure people pause more often in their speech. Can you find the most nervous person here?
    ● How does the parent make it clear that she is less than impressed?

5   **Who uses specialist language?** We can confuse and intimidate people by choosing to use technical language. How does the administrator attempt to impress with jargon? Does he do it well enough to hide his hesitation?

6   **Who decides what is right or wrong**? The headteacher tries to draw the situation to a close by concluding and closing down the discussion. Which of her statements show this most clearly?

GradeStudio

Examiner tips

● Use highlighters to colour-code your transcript for different features.
● It will probably help if you work with a partner on your transcript and ask your teacher for guidance.
● Work through your transcript, commenting and explaining in detail.
● Bring out the features of spoken language in your answer, focusing on language choices that suit the listener, using examples.
● Write about what is said but also **how** it is said.

GradeStudio

Here are two extracts from student responses to the sample question about language choice using the transcript on page 162. Read the answers together with the examiner comments, then check what you have learnt and try putting it into practice.

Show that you understand the significance of the language choices made by people with and without authority. (20 marks)

C grade answer

Student 1

From the opening of the essay
The headteacher and the administrator have the authority here and they plot together before they start to talk to the parent, 'try and get some really good facts (.) throw her off OK (3)'.
The mother has come in to complain about the food that her son has to eat and the two school employees are ganging up to tell her that everything is OK.

From the middle paragraphs of the essay
The mother uses quite posh English to make her complaint. 'I am appalled at the standard of food served in your school.' The headteacher replies by observing that she has nothing to do with the food, which drops her colleague right in it!

From the ending of the essay
The administrator tries to impress the mother with the quality of the food, 'high quality from trusted and inspected farmers around the country, ... the food is pre-prepared and brought in.' The headteacher follows up 'it's absolutely perfect food' and the mother has to give in.

> Some good understanding here and evidence in support

> 'Posh English' is ok but stops any development or detail.

> Again, the words are understood but the pauses and hesitations are missed.

Examiner comment

This answer identifies accurately the authority of the headteacher and the administrator and their working together and preparations, but ignores the power that a parent can have. The headteacher's quiet 'waste of time' is ignored. The tone and language used by the mother is identified as 'posh' but more detail would be helpful (the choice of 'appalled' and the formal 'I am here today'). The answer misses the way the headteacher echoes the parent's words, so gets what is said but not how it is said. The same is true of the administrator's words, which are delivered in a hesitant, uncertain way. This answer misinterprets the result and assumes that the parent has lost. C grade.

Language choice: how to go up the grades

To move up the grades you need to focus specifically on the language choices made, suggesting why similar words are less effective in that context. So the choice of 'appalled' by the mother and 'waste of time' by the headteacher is a key part of the grade A answer. Another key focus in better answers is keeping conclusions tentative. The mother's choice of response to the headteacher's weak excuses is well worth commenting on. Seeing some of the more subtle points will also move you up the grades. Once again, frequent use of key quotations always helps.

Student 2

<u>From the opening of the essay</u>

The headteacher and the administrator have some authority here but they are clearly worried about the parent's power and so plot together and try to dismiss her, 'waste of time'. You can tell they are a bit afraid because they say it 'very quietly'. The mother has come in to complain about the food that her son has to eat and although she is quite indignant she won't let her son say anything even though he ate the food!

> A strong start picking up some subtle ideas about the context.

> Attention is given to the behaviour of the son.

<u>From the middle paragraphs of the essay</u>

The mother chooses quite formal English to make her complaint, 'I am appalled at the standard of food served in your school.' She chooses 'appalled' rather than a word like 'disgusted' or 'sick' because it is formal Standard English and not heard very often.

> The focus on choice is strong here.

<u>From the ending of the essay</u>

The administrator also tries to impress the mother 'our food is of high quality' but his hesitations and frequent pauses undermine his attempts to sound convincing. The parent clearly isn't impressed. 'Huh'. The head teacher tries to support her colleague 'it's absolutely perfect food' but isn't very convincing as she has already admitted that she has very little to do with it. The ending is not conclusive, but the mother is forceful and dominant and so will probably win.

> Good detail here on the language choices.

Examiner comment

This answer is much clearer on the language choices and the reasons for them. The awareness and understanding are clear from the opening analysis of 'waste of time'. Word choices are highlighted and discussed ('appalled'). This answer again looks not only at what is said but also how it is said ('hesitations and frequent pauses'). This would get a grade A.

Putting it into practice

You have learnt that language choices are used to suit different listeners. You have explored language choices in a situation involving authority and also the qualities of an A grade answer.

Use what you have learnt when you look at language choice in any context, and use these **key questions** to help you.

- Who is making the language choices?
- What kind of choice are they making?
- Who is choosing a style furthest from their usual one?
- Who is most at ease in the style of language used? Who least?

When writing your essay, remember to:

- quote examples from the transcript to support your ideas
- be tentative when writing conclusions, e.g. 'this **could** be because he lacks confidence'
- start by writing about the language choices
- include the expectations of listeners.

- to understand the effects of standard and non-standard spoken language
- to analyse a transcript and demonstrate how standard and non-standard language may vary over time and place.

Language variation

Examiner tip

Always use these key questions of language variation:
- What forms of standard and non-standard speech are being used?
- What effects are these varieties of speech having?
- How is speech being adapted here?

Language variation is how we vary between standard and non-standard ways of speaking (for example we might speak in dialect, crude slang with friends and formal language with a teacher). To demonstrate how standard and non-standard language is used and may vary over time and place, it is useful to explore situations where choice is important. For example, in speaking to family or peers we may use non-standard forms that include slang and more informal language. If we are speaking to strangers or those in authority, we may use standard forms that are more formal and polite.

Below is a brief example of the kind of approach you might take, using the following sample question.

Choose a situation where the use of a standard or non-standard language variety is important. Explain why speakers may use standard and non-standard language at different times and places.

Activity 1

Read the question above and the transcripts opposite. The transcripts show how a speaker has chosen to vary her use of non-standard and standard forms of spoken language in an informal and formal situation. Explore the way the language has been varied by completing a table like the one below.

Non-standard spoken language (to friends)	Standard spoken language (to teacher)	Variation	
it were well good	I had a really good time	Non-standard language including dialect features 'it were' rather than 'it was' and 'well' as an adjective instead of 'really' or 'very'	Local words that define you as coming from a particular place.
they let me 'ave a go at all the jobs	they let me try out all of the jobs	Non-standard language including accent dropping the initial 'h'. Standard language to impress the teacher	Local accent, which is the way you make your sounds. Melissa doesn't sound the 'g' sound in 'banging' and the 'h' in 'have'. That is accent.
for a coupla days	for two days	Non-standard language, running words together. Informal and probably excited. Standard language to be specific with the teacher	
pressie	I really enjoyed that		
	because		
I had a bangin time			

Non-standard spoken language: Melissa, a Manchester schoolgirl, telling her friends about her work experience.

aw yer (.) it were <u>well good</u> (.) they let
me 'ave a go at <u>all</u> the jobs n'everything
(.) and they treated me just like one o'
them (.) I got to work in the office for a bit
5 (.) then I was out on t'delivery van for a
coupla days (1) <u>that</u> were top (.) then on
the last day like they took me out to a <u>well</u>
<u>good</u> restaurant cos I'd slaved away like (.)
and they bought me lunch cos they said I
10 were (.) like (.) one of them really <u>and</u> gave
me a pressie (1) they said they <u>might</u> even
have a job for me when I leave school (.)
I had a bangin time it were <u>great</u>

Standard spoken language: Melissa telling her form teacher about her work experience.

yes (.) I had a <u>really</u> good time Miss (.)
they didn't just make me do photocopying
(.) they let me try out <u>all</u> of the jobs and
treated me like a <u>proper</u> worker (.) I really
5 enjoyed it (.) I worked in the office for
two days and then I had two days out on
deliveries so I could experience <u>that</u> as
well (.) I <u>really</u> enjoyed that (.) then on
the last day they took me out for a lunch
10 because they said I'd worked so <u>hard</u> and
they weren't allowed to pay me <u>and</u> they
gave me a present (.) some vouchers too
(.) I <u>really</u> enjoyed it Miss (.) and they said
they <u>might</u> even have a job for me when I
15 leave school

GradeStudio

Here are two student responses to the sample exam question below. Read the answers together with the examiner comments, then check what you have learnt and try putting it into practice.

Choose a situation where the use of a standard or non-standard language variety is important. Explain why speakers may use standard and non-standard language at different times and places. (20 marks)

C grade answer

Student 1

<u>From the opening of the essay</u>
In this transcript Melissa is talking to her friends about her work experience. She is quite excited about it and that is making her jumble her words and not speak properly. For example she says 'yer' not 'yes' which is a bit sloppy and wrong. She runs quite a lot of her words together. Maybe she just talks fast.

> Good opening. Gets the mood well. Aware of some language features.

<u>From the middle of the essay</u>
When she talks to her teacher Melissa goes all posh. She seems to want to impress her teacher and is quite polite, 'miss'. She clearly can talk properly when she wants to. She doesn't shorten her words either, she says 'present', not 'pressie' and uses harder words like 'experience'.

> Some good selection of words. Good on wanting to impress.

<u>From the end of the essay</u>
Melissa says, 'like' a lot which I suppose is a northern thing as they say it on 'Coronation Street' but she doesn't say it to her teacher who would probably tell her off. Melissa's mates probably all talk like her so they would understand what she is saying.

> Misses the idea that Melissa can vary her language.

Examiner comment

This student has a good try at the two transcripts and uses several examples, which is good. She doesn't seem to realise though, that Melissa, like everyone else, can vary her language to fit in. The candidate is not aware either that you can impress some people by using standard language, and others by using non-standard. She is broadly aware of the Manchester accent but doesn't identify slang, accent or dialect. Grade C.

A **grade answer**

Student 2

<u>From the opening of the essay</u>
Melissa is a Manchester student and like lots of people she likes to fit in with her friends. She does this in the first transcript by talking the way her friends do. She is very excited and wants to impress them so she says 'it were well good'. My Mum would tell me off for saying this but I say it to my friends. I think it is slang because it is a young person's style of language.

<u>From the middle part of the essay</u>
Melissa varies her language when talking to her teacher. She wants to impress her teacher with what she did on work experience, but also uses language that is closer to how the teacher herself talks. She says 'I really enjoyed it' three times but doesn't slip in any of her slang terms.

<u>From the end of the essay</u>
Melissa really says much the same thing in both these transcripts. The difference is that she uses standard language to her teacher and non-standard to her friends. Non-standard is 'cooler' to her friends and she uses a mix of Manchester accent 't'delivery van' and trendy slang 'a well good restaurant'. Melissa speaks at least two varieties of English.

> Aware of one of the main reasons we use slang. Good.

> Sensible comments. Aware that standard speech is another variety.

Examiner summary

This candidate shows good awareness of the reasons we all have for using non-standard forms. S/he relates Melissa's language varieties to his/her own speech and identifies slang clearly, and understands the idea of local speech. In the middle of the essay the candidate recognises that standard speech is another variety and we all choose to use it at certain times. The ending of the essay is strong because it recognises that Melissa is saying essentially the same thing in both transcripts. There is recognition of accent and slang and both are identified correctly. Grade A.

Language variation: how to go up the grades

To move up the grades it is important to recognise that we all speak several varieties of English and that non-standard language is the right variety in some circumstances. Understanding the reasons and effects for using standard and non-standard speech is important. Moving away from a wrong/right focus is important. Identifying and seeing the difference between slang, accent and dialect is another important factor in moving up the grades. If you are not sure about a language feature or exactly why someone is speaking in a certain way, it is more accurate to be a little tentative: use 'may' or 'might' – after all, sometimes we just don't know.

Putting it into practice

You have learnt that language varies over time and place and that standard and non-standard varieties are used to suit different situations and roles. You have explored language varieties based around a work experience context and also the qualities of a C grade answer and an A grade answer.

Use what you have learnt when you look at language varieties in any context, and use these **key questions** to help you:

- What forms of standard and non-standard speech are being used?
- What effects are these varieties of speech having?
- How is speech being adapted here?

Answer **all** the following questions.

The resource material (pages 171–173) for use in this paper is a newspaper article by Joanna Walters from the *Daily Express* and an extract from the *New York Times* by Ian Fisher which appeared on the Internet.

Question 1

Look at the first part of the newspaper article by Joanna Walters on page 171.

What do you learn from this part of the article about the inmates of Lakeview Shock Prison and the way they are treated? **(10)**

Question 2

Now look at the rest of the article by Joanna Walters on pages 171–172.

What impressions does Joanne Walters give of Sean Clarke and Eric Flowers? **(10)**

Question 3

Now look at 'Prison Boot Camps Prove No Sure Cure' on page 173.

How does this text try to show that the boot camp prison is 'no sure cure'? **(10)**

Question 4

To answer this question you will need to look at both texts.

Compare and contrast what these two texts say about Lakeview Shock Prison. **(10)**

You should organise your answer into two paragraphs, using the following headings:
- the advantages of the 'shock' system
- the effect of the 'shock' system on the inmates.

Daily Express

ISN'T THIS THE SORT OF JAIL BRITAIN NEEDS?

It is 5.45 am and 250 men and 50 women are on their backs on a rain-drenched physical training yard doing sit-ups. 'Lakeview. Shock!' they chant in unison, counting out exercises during 45 minutes of press-ups, crunches, star jumps and lunges. They wear regulation shorts and T-shirts while drill instructors
5 keep order.

The workout ends with the 300 yelling on command: 'Fired up, fired up, fired up SIR! Motivated, motivated, motivated, SIR!'

This session is to be followed by a six-mile run, jogged platoon by platoon, in step. Around them, rolls of razor wire are glinting in the rising sun.

10 This is not the Army, this is a prison and the 300 crop-headed individuals are just some of the 1,400 inmates at this penitentiary, serving their sentence in a highly-effective form of boot camp known in America as the Shock Incarceration Programme (SIP). This is a jail of which there is no equivalent in Britain, however much many people may wish it to stem our ever-spiralling
15 crime figures.

It specialises in shaking up criminals convicted of offences such as burglary, theft, joyriding and drug-dealing where they did not use violence but are a menace to society. It tries to turn them away from a life of crime into responsible citizens, using a mix of military discipline, compulsory education and drug
20 treatment.

'These offenders are committing what we often call gateway crimes that, unless stopped, will usually lead to more horrendous behaviour,' says Ronald Moscicki, superintendent of Lakeview Shock Prison in upstate New York, the state with the largest such programme in America. New York jails up to 90 per
25 cent of its burglars, car thieves and drug dealers for at least two years, even for first offences, but some can be out in six months if they choose – and then can endure – the Shock programme.

Lakeview makes prisoners get up at 5.30am during the week, 6am at weekends, with no day off for six months, PT every day, work, chores, education
30 and Alcoholics Anonymous-style substance-abuse rehabilitation, uniform pressing, marching and constant evaluation. Inmates lead a spartan existence without television, magazines or recreation.

Sitting in the mess hall, soaked after PT, wolfing a breakfast of corned beef hash and eggs before showering, are Sean Clarke and Eric Flowers, two typical

35 convicts. While most inmates report for 'hard labour' after breakfast, they will complete their sentence that day. 'I started getting into trouble when I was about 11 or 12. I was very selfish and I needed prison a long time ago,' says Clarke, 26. His father is a Londoner but his mother is American and he was born in New York. He burgled shops, bars, laundrettes and other businesses at night, stealing

40 the safes to fund his cocaine habit, and binge drinking. Some of his friends were housebreakers and he was arrested for driving their getaway car.

Instead of serving the mandated sentence of between two-and-a-half and seven years in ordinary prison, he pleaded guilty quickly and asked to take the six-month Shock as punishment because his wife was pregnant.

45 'My first thought was not about changing but about getting out as soon as possible but as I went through boot camp, I learnt a lot about myself,' he says.

Plastered with tattoos but lean and healthy with a neat haircut, a steady gaze and a shirt and tie, Clarke is looking forward to freedom and a new life of integrity.

50 'I was a know-it-all when I got here, but after getting into a fight and spending 30 days in solitary confinement in December, including Christmas, in an 8ft-by-8ft cell we call The Box, I changed my tune,' he admits.

Clarke and Flowers have jobs lined up. As a condition of parole, an ex-Shock inmate must work, or attend job training or college. Ironically, the programme

55 is so well-known for turning hoodlums into keen workers grateful for a second chance that many employers request them.

Clarke is a cement and concrete labourer. Flowers, 20, from the small town of Batavia in upstate New York, had just qualified as a welder when he was arrested for stealing copper wire with a 'bad lot' of friends.

60 'I feel very ashamed of myself and what I did. I was horrible,' he says.

Coming to Lakeview Shock Prison was, indeed, a shock. 'We got on the bus from the ordinary prison and, immediately, drill instructors were yelling in your face, letting you know who was in charge. I was scared. It's tough here, any time you do the slightest thing wrong, they punish you. In the end, you

65 learn to keep quiet and do as you are told.'

The New York Times

Prison Boot Camps Prove No Sure Cure

No-one complained at 5.45 this morning when a drill instructor shouted for another round of push-ups on the cold and wet pavement wriggling with worms that
5 crawled from the newly thawed earth. But a few hours later, 38 young inmates sat in a circle and spoke uneasily about the final task in this gruelling boot camp prison: they had to go home.

10 'My name is Mr Cooper,' a drug dealer from New York City told other inmates here a day before his release from Lakeview Shock Incarceration Facility, half a mile from Lake Erie. 'I'm not ... I'm excited but I'm scared.
15 I've got to do it on my own. It's about time I grew up.'

After six months of pre-dawn runs, military drills, drug treatment and clean living, Randy Cooper's fear of returning to crime seemed
20 justified: despite completing a programme that many criminal-justice experts once hoped would solve every problem from overcrowding to reforming young offenders, he is no more likely over time to stay out
25 of trouble than an inmate who served his sentence in a regular prison.

The paradox for New York State's boot camp programme, at a time when many justice experts and politicians are questioning
30 the value of such boot camps around the nation, is that the state's programme is considered one of the best. Inmates do not simply move rocks; they attend daily substance-abuse classes, group therapy sessions and academic training courses, 35 and are closely monitored in an intensive six-month programme to be completed after leaving boot camp.

Yet the dropout rate is high; about a quarter of the inmates fail to complete the programme 40 and are sent to a regular prison. And although boot camp graduates do marginally better than other inmates at first, after two years the numbers of offenders who return to prison are roughly the same, around 50% over four 45 years. [...]

Defenders of boot camps [...] say expectations were too high from the start. There is no single quick fix, they say, that can overcome the problems of 50 violence, drugs and family dissolution that especially infest New York City's poorest neighbourhoods. [...]

Moreover, in New York, though not in every state, boot camps have met other 55 goals: saving money and reducing prison overcrowding. Officials in New York, which has the nation's largest boot camp programme, with more than 1,800 beds, estimate the programme has saved $305 60 million [...] because inmates serve shorter sentences, freeing beds for other convicts.

Answer Question 1 **and** Question 2

In this section you will be assessed for your writing skills, including the presentation of your work. Take special care with handwriting, spelling and punctuation.

Think about the purpose, audience and, where appropriate, the format for your writing.

A guide to the amount you should write is given at the end of each question.

1   A company that runs play-schemes for children in the 3–10 age range is looking to recruit part-time staff for the school summer holidays.

   You decide to apply.

   Write your letter of application.   (20)

   The quality of your writing is more important than its length. You should write about one to two pages in your answer book.

2   You have to give a talk to your class with the title 'Mobile Phones: a blessing or a curse?'

   Write what you would say.   (20)

   The quality of your writing is more important than its length. You should write about one to two pages in your answer book.